John Carroll

PROJECT 2007

In easy steps is an imprint of Computer Step
Southfield Road · Southam
Warwickshire CV47 0FB · United Kingdom
www.ineasysteps.com

Notice of Liability
Every effort has been made to ensure that this book contains accurate
and current information. However, Computer Step and the author
shall not be liable for any loss or damage suffered by readers as a
result of any information contained herein.

Trademarks
Microsoft® and Windows® are registered trademarks of Microsoft
Corporation. All other trademarks are acknowledged as belonging to
their respective companies.

Printed and bound in the United Kingdom

ISBN-13 978-1-84078-325-4
ISBN-10 1-84078-325-7

Contents

5   Adding Structure   59

6   More About Tasks   71

7   Resources   83

8   Project Costs   95

9 Project Calendars — 107

10 Project Scheduling — 119

11 Conflicts and Constraints — 129

12 Viewing Data — 145

13   Printing Reports   161

14   Tracking Progress   171

Index   187

1 The Basics

This chapter introduces Microsoft Office Project 2007 and explains how it can help you manage your projects. It also introduces the concepts of project management and how they can help ensure your projects are successful.

Introduction

Microsoft Office Project 2007 (whether you have the Standard or Professional version) is a great project management tool. Managing projects can be a complex activity but, with the help of Project, you can plan, schedule and track the progress of your project, so that you stay in control.

The Standard and Professional versions of Project are effectively the same when used in "stand-alone" mode and this book covers both. In addition to the functionality of the Standard version, the Professional version allows you to collaborate and share information with other Project users in your organization, through the use of a companion product, Project Server.

Whether your project is a simple short-term one (such as arranging a company event) or a more complex project (like launching a new product), Project 2007 can help you stay in control of it.

Project 2007 Features

Used as a planning tool, Project 2007 can produce some great looking charts and diagrams to help you plan your project. But Project can do a lot more besides:

- It can help you to understand, develop and manage project plans and schedules

- It can produce a critical path analysis to identify the areas where you will need to keep a close track on progress

- It can identify if you have too much work allocated to any one person

- It can schedule facilities, such as meeting rooms and equipment for you

- It can help you to understand and control project budgets and costs

- It can keep track of public holidays and team members' vacations

- It can help you build professional looking reports to communicate and present project information in an effective and understandable way

Beware

The examples and illustrations in this book are of Project 2007. If you are using an earlier version some features may look different or may not be available. The main differences are annotated in warnings like this.

Project Management

Successful project management is about completing a project on time, within budget and with the needs of the business fully met. But while this is easy to say, a recent survey found that half of the projects companies launch end up failing. Other surveys have found that, depending on how you define failure, it could be as little as 25% (total failure) or as much as 75% if you add the total failures and significantly challenged.

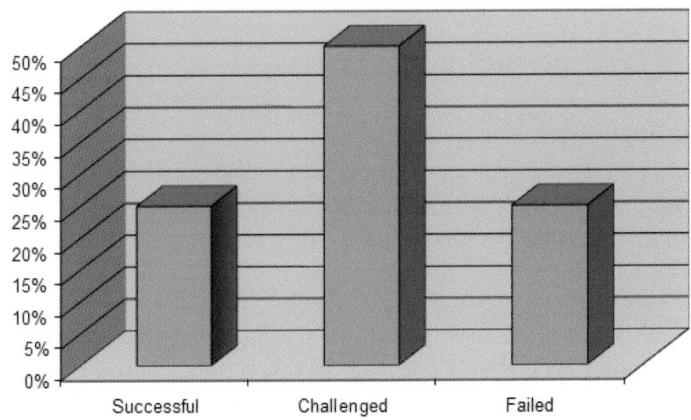

Whichever way you look at it, only around one quarter of projects end up as fully successful (i.e. completed on time, within budget and with the required scope). In order to get most projects completed, corners have to be cut, but things still seem to take longer than expected. As a further result, costs inevitably seem to increase.

Successful Projects

It doesn't have to be that way. We know how to ensure projects are successful and it's not rocket science, it's just plain common sense. Throughout this book, you will find some basic project management concepts that have been proved in practice. Follow these concepts and advice to ensure that your project will be successful.

Microsoft Project

Project 2007 is a great product that will help you plan, organize and control your project. It won't carry it out for you (you still have to do that yourself), but what it will do is help you to control it and complete it successfully.

Hot tip

The Project Management concepts, advice and tips in this book are all listed in the index under Concepts.

What's New?

There are a number of minor changes and enhancements in Project 2007, which are noted where relevant throughout the book. The key new features and functionality are:

Task Drivers

For any task, this facility shows the prerequisite tasks and any resource constraints that can affect the task's start date. Just click the link to display the relevant information and keep on top of your project tasks.

Visual Change Highlights

Any time you make a change to your project that change will be highlighted together with any other tasks that are dependant on and affected by the change. You can instantly see the full impact of a change and, with Multiple Level Undo (the next new feature) immediately correct any mistakes.

In the following example the duration of Task One has been increased from one to two days. This is highlighted along with the start dates of tasks three, four, six and seven, which have been put back by one day as a result of the change:

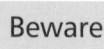

Beware

Please note that the dates illustrated in this book are in MM/DD/YY format.

	Task Name	Duration	Start
1	Task One	2 days	Mon 7/2/07
2	Task Two	2 days	Mon 7/2/07
3	Task Three	1 day	Wed 7/4/07
4	Task Four	3 days	Thu 7/5/07
5	Task Five	1 day	Wed 7/4/07
6	Task Six	4 days	Tue 7/10/07
7	Task Seven	2 days	Mon 7/16/07

Multiple Level Undo

This is the long-awaited ability to undo a series of changes rather than just the last change made (which was a restriction in all previous versions of Project). This not only allows you to back out a series of changes but, together with Visual Change Highlights, (above) will also allow you to explore "what if" scenarios on your project.

Predefined Financial Fields

New financial fields, such as cost codes, allow much easier tracking of financial information in a project. They also allow Project to be mapped to a full project accounting system.

Budget Tracking

This new feature allows the definition of a high-level budget for a project (or even for a programme) against which funds can be allocated and costs can be tracked for improved financial control.

Cost Resources

In addition to the existing people and material resources, the introduction of cost resources allow planned and actual costs to be assigned and tracked by task. This feature also supports the integration of Project 2007 to a full accounting system.

Visual Reports

Project 2007 now allows you to export project-related data to Microsoft Office Word (for documents), Excel (for charts and spreadsheets), PowerPoint (for presentations) and Visio (for diagrams). You can also export project data to custom defined Excel and Visio templates to produce charts, graphs and diagrams based on project data. This includes the ability to produce a three-dimensional data cube for advanced drill-downs and pivot tables.

Background Cell Highlighting

You can now shade cells, in a similar way to Excel, in order to highlight or convey additional meaning, as shown in the following illustration:

	Task Name	Duration	Start	Finish	Jul 2, '07	Jul 9, '07
					S M T W T F S	S M T W T F S
1	Task One	2 days	Mon 7/2/07	Tue 7/3/07		
2	Task Two	2 days	Mon 7/2/07	Tue 7/3/07		
3	Task Three	1 day	Wed 7/4/07	Wed 7/4/07		
4	Task Four	3 days	Thu 7/5/07	Mon 7/9/07		
5	Task Five	1 day	Wed 7/4/07	Wed 7/4/07		
6	Task Six	4 days	Tue 7/10/07	Fri 7/13/07		
7	Task Seven	2 days	Mon 7/16/07	Tue 7/17/07		
8						

Calendar Interface

The calendar interface has been significantly enhanced to make working with project and resource calendars much more flexible and intuitive.

The calendar interface together with all of the other new features are fully explained under their own topics in this book. For more details on any of these new features, check the Table of Contents or Index.

Installing Project

Beware

You will need 2GB of free disk space to install Project, but some of this will be freed up after installation. The setup program will warn you if you do not have enough room.

Installing Microsoft Office Project 2007 is straightforward. If you are installing from a CD, the setup program will usually run automatically when the CD is inserted into the drive. If it doesn't start, use Windows Explorer to locate the setup program (called setup.exe) and double-click on it.

Setup

The first thing that Setup will do is ask for the product key, so make sure you have this to hand before you start. The product key is usually on a sticker on the back of the CD case or it should have been provided to you with the software if it was distributed under a volume licensing agreement.

1. Start the installation by inserting the CD or double-clicking the setup program (setup.exe)

2. When asked, enter the product key and click Continue

3. The setup program will display the license terms. You will need to select Accept the license terms and click on Continue

4. Choose Install Now and setup will carry on and install Project 2007. Once installation is complete you will be offered the option of registering for online services

5. To register for online services click on Go to Office Online and select Register Now to be taken to the Microsoft registration website, where you will be guided through the registration process. If you don't want to register at this time just click on Close to complete the installation process

Don't forget

You can always register at a later date if you do not want to do it immediately (see Getting Started for details).

While it is not essential to register for Microsoft Online Services, it can provide automatic updates and other useful services. If you don't wish to do it now you can always do it later, see the Getting Started topic towards the end of this chapter for details.

You have now completed the installation process but you will also need to activate the product (see the next topic).

Activating Project

Microsoft Project needs to be activated. You don't have to do this straight away, as it will allow you to run it up to 50 times before you have to activate it. It will keep reminding you during this period, but it is usually best to do it as soon as possible.

Activation Wizard

Unless your software was pre-activated, the first time you open the program the activation wizard will appear asking you how you want to activate the software:

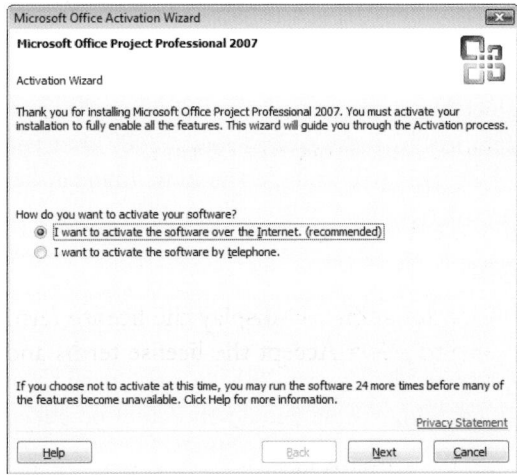

1. Activate over the Internet is the default option and is the most straightforward to use as long as you have Internet access. Select this option and click Next to complete the activation process online

2. If you don't have Internet access, select activate by telephone and click Next. You will be given instructions for completing the process by telephone

3. If you do not wish to complete the activation process at this time, click Cancel and you can continue to use Project up to 50 times before you need to activate it

Once you have completed the activation process you will see a confirmation screen with the option of going to Office online to register (see the previous topic for details).

 Hot tip

Each time you start up Project, it will warn you how many more times you can use it before activation.

Backward Compatibility

While Project 2007 provides some significant enhancements over earlier versions of Project, Microsoft have maintained backward compatibility with these earlier versions back as far as Project 98. This means that you can open project files created in earlier versions of Project and also save files back in these earlier formats.

However, because the new and enhanced features introduced in Project 2000, 2002, 2003 and 2007, are not supported in earlier versions, there could be some unexpected results. Any features that did not exist in an earlier version will simply be discarded if a file is saved back into that earlier format.

Project 2002/2003

When a project file is saved in Project 2002 or 2003 format, any of the new features introduced in Project 2007 that you have used will be lost. This will include the new financial fields, budget tracking and cost resources.

Project 2000

Versions after Project 2000 include refinements to the scheduling engine that improve performance and precision. This can affect project plans created in Project 2000 in two areas: Earned Value Analysis and Tracking. These should therefore be checked the first time a project is opened in Project 2007.

When a project file is saved in Project 2000 format, any later features will be lost. In addition to the items listed for Project 2002/2003 above, multiple baselines and some of the earned value fields will also be lost. Task constraints may also be lost if the project has been updated and rescheduled in Project 2007.

Project 98

In addition to the issues listed above, it is possible for schedule dates to change the first time a file, created in Project 98, is opened in Project 2007. It is also possible that some tasks may move on or off the critical path due to the different way in which it is now calculated. For these reasons the project schedule should be checked the first time it is opened in Project 2007.

When saving files in Project 98 format: deadline dates, estimated duration and material resources will all be lost, in addition to the details listed above for the later versions.

Hot tip

Always check the project schedule the first time you open a file created in Project 2000 or 98.

The Gantt Chart

The first thing you see when you open or create a new project is the Gantt chart.

It is the default view, and with good reason. The Gantt chart is probably the most widely used and most useful project management tool.

They say that every picture tells a thousand words and this is the key picture in your project:

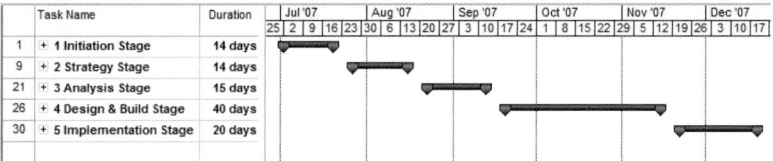

	Task Name	Duration	Jul '07	Aug '07	Sep '07	Oct '07	Nov '07	Dec '07
1	+ 1 Initiation Stage	14 days						
9	+ 2 Strategy Stage	14 days						
21	+ 3 Analysis Stage	15 days						
26	+ 4 Design & Build Stage	40 days						
30	+ 5 Implementation Stage	20 days						

At the summary-level (as illustrated above) you can view the whole project on one screen or sheet of paper. The Gantt chart represents the most frequently used way of representing a project graphically and is particularly useful for senior management in its rolled-up summary form as above.

At the more detailed-level (as illustrated below), the Gantt chart is typically used by the project manager and project team to communicate and track project progress, by task, on a day-to-day basis.

	Task Name	Duration	Start	Jul 2, '07	Jul 9, '07	Jul 16, '07
1	− 1 Initiation Stage	14 days	Mon 7/2/07			
2	1.1 Agree Project Objectives	1 day	Mon 7/2/07	Prudence Project		
3	1.2 Identify Stakeholders	1 day	Tue 7/3/07	Prudence Project		
4	1.3 Identify Project Team	2 days	Wed 7/4/07	Bill Buggs,Prudence Project		
5	1.4 Identify Business Case	1 day	Mon 7/9/07		Prudence Project,Bill Buggs	
6	1.5 Analyse the Risks	1 day	Wed 7/11/07		Prudence Project	
7	1.6 Produce Outline Project Plan	1 day	Thu 7/12/07		Prudence Project	
8	1.7 Project Approval	0 days	Thu 7/19/07			7/19
9	+ 2 Strategy Stage	14 days	Fri 7/27/07			
21	+ 3 Analysis Stage	15 days	Thu 8/23/07			
26	+ 4 Design & Build Stage	40 days	Thu 9/20/07			

In addition to letting you view the project schedule at the strategic (high-level) and operational (detailed-level), the Gantt chart view also allows you to insert and edit tasks and allocate the people and other resources to work on the tasks. You can set milestones and deadlines and generally keep track of your project and the resources working on it.

View Bar

While the Gantt Chart view is the default (and probably the most useful) view in Project 2007, there are another 25 predefined views, that can be selected through the View Bar. This can be seen down the left-hand side in the illustration below.

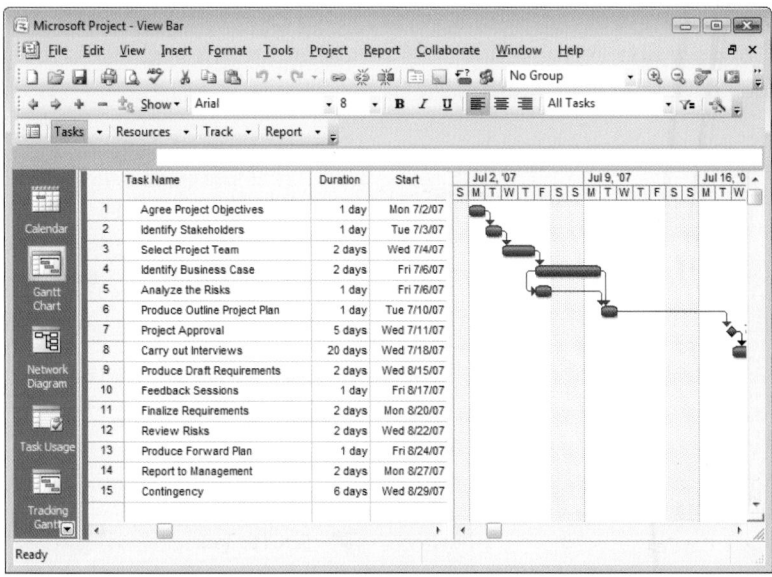

The View Bar can be used to switch back and forth between different views. These are the views available on the view bar:

- Calendar: a monthly calendar showing tasks and their duration

- Gantt Chart: the default view of tasks and time lines

- Network Diagram: a chart of tasks showing links and dependencies

- Task Usage: tasks with the resources allocated to them

- Tracking Gantt: showing actual progress against schedule

- Resource Graph: showing the usage or cost of resources over time

- Resource Usage: list of task assignments by resource name

- More Views: full list of all 26 available views

Toolbars

The standard and formatting toolbars contain the usual Microsoft Office buttons together with a number of additional Project specific buttons:

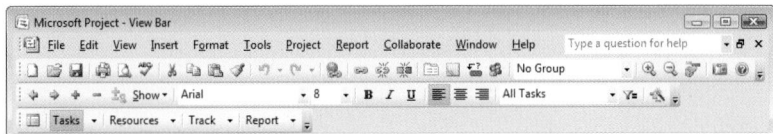

Buttons

The principal standard and formatting buttons, with their specific functionality within Project 2007, is as follows:

New	Ctrl+N	
Open...	Ctrl+O	
Save	Ctrl+S	
Print	Ctrl+P	
Print Preview		
Spelling...	F7	
Cut Cell	Ctrl+X	
Copy Cell	Ctrl+C	
Paste	Ctrl+V	
Format Painter		
Undo		
Redo		
Hyperlink...	Ctrl+K	
Link Tasks	Ctrl+F2	
Unlink Tasks	Ctrl+Shift+F2	
Split Task		
Task Information...	Shift+F2	

Task Notes...		
Task Drivers		
Assign Resources...	Alt+F10	
Group By:		
Zoom In	Ctrl+/	
Zoom Out	Ctrl+*	
Scroll to Task	Ctrl+Shift+F5	
Copy Picture...		
Microsoft Office Project Help	F1	
Outdent	Alt+Shift+Left	
Indent	Alt+Shift+Right	
Show Subtasks	Alt+Shift+Plus	
Hide Subtasks	Alt+Shift+Minus	
Hide Assignments		
Show		
AutoFilter		
Gantt Chart Wizard...		

Don't forget

You can always find out what any button does by pausing the pointer over it.

Hot tip

If you don't see all of these buttons you can use Toolbar Options to show any others.

1   To list the buttons on a toolbar, with their functions (as in the above illustrations), click on Toolbar Options (the down arrow at the right-hand end of each toolbar) and then select "Add or Remove Buttons"

2   To add or remove toolbars select View>Toolbars from the Menu bar (above the toolbars)

Getting Help

1 Select Help>Microsoft Office Project Help from the Menu bar (or press the F1 key) to bring up the Help screen

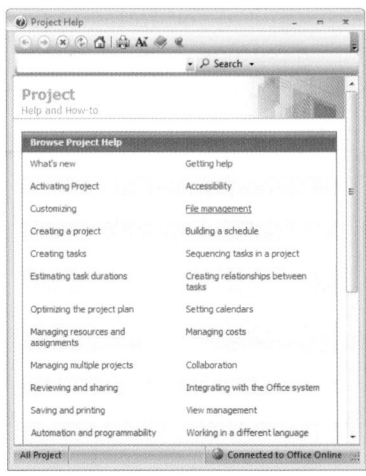

2 Click on the subject you would like help on (e.g. File Management) to bring up a list of the available sub-categories of help

3 Select the required sub-category and the required help text will be displayed

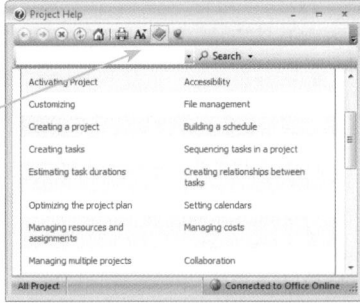

4 Click on Show Table of Contents to bring up the table of contents in a separate pane to the left of the help screen (as below)

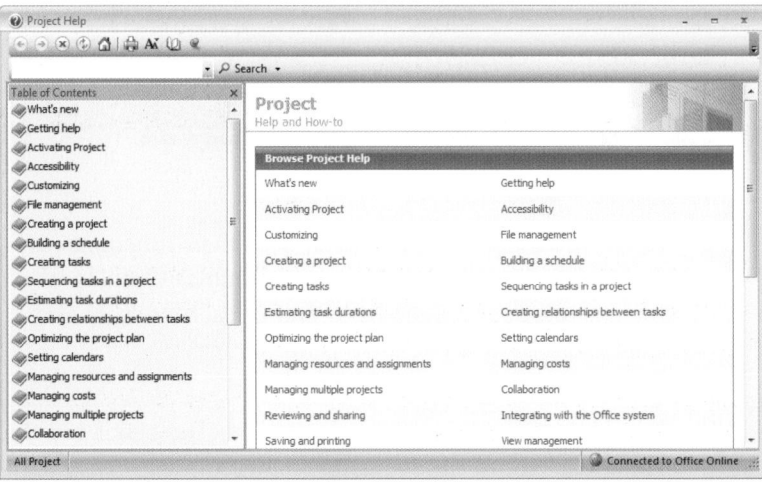

Getting Started

For more information about Project and lots of helpful advice and guidance, Microsoft provide Microsoft Office Online. As long as you have Internet access this can be accessed through the Help menu:

1. Click on Help>Microsoft Office Online and the Welcome page is displayed

2. If you didn't register when you installed Project you can do so now by clicking on Sign up now

3. Select the Products tab and then click on Project for access to all the available Project Online services:

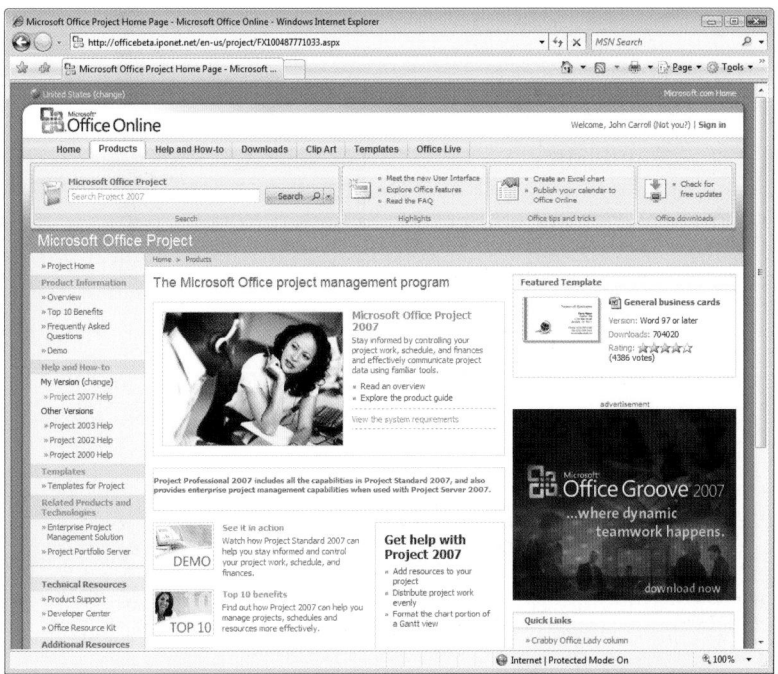

From here you can read an overview of Project, take a tour of the key features, access project templates, download add-ins and product updates, obtain support and provide feedback.

If you bookmark this site in your web browser you don't even have to be in Project to access it in future.

Summary

- Microsoft Project 2007 can help you to plan and schedule your project, allocate tasks and track progress and costs

- One thing Project can't do for you is manage the actual work of your project. Around 50% of projects fail for reasons that are known and understood. This book includes some proven project management concepts to make sure your project is a success

- Project 2007 introduces some new functionality: Task Drivers, Visual Change Highlighting, Multi-level Undo, Predefined Financial Fields, Budget Tracking, Cost Resources, Visual Reporting, Background Cell Highlighting and an improved Calendar Interface. These are all covered in detail under the relevant topics in this book

- Installing Project is a straightforward process as long as you have your product key to hand. Once installed, Project also needs to be activated (via the Internet is easiest) but you can run it up to 50 times before doing so

- You can transfer project files, in both directions, between Project 2007 and earlier versions (as far back as Project 98) but any new features you have used will be lost when saving a file in an earlier format

- The Gantt chart is the most useful view in Project and the one in which you will probably choose to do most of your work

- The View Bar allows you to switch between different views with a single mouse click

- Project is fully compatible with the standard Microsoft Office menu, toolbars and buttons but it also contains its own specialized functionality, such as Indent and Outdent

- Getting help is only a click away or you can use the F1 key

- Microsoft Office Online contains some useful tutorial and other information to help you get started with Project. You can also download Project templates, add-ins and updates, and obtain support

2 Project Guide

The Project Guide provides a simple way to set up and get started with a project. It gives detailed instruction on how to perform some basic project activities.

Project Guide

The Project Guide provides a quick and easy way to start creating a project using fairly basic functionality. It is ideal for people new to Microsoft Project and those with no previous experience of project management. It consists of three main components:

1 The toolbar displays the top-level navigation buttons called the goal areas (Tasks, Resources, Track and Report). Click on any of these to bring the goal area into view in the side panel (see next step)

2 The side panel is displayed on the left-hand side of the screen and is used for navigation within each of the goal areas. The initial side panel for the Task goal area is illustrated on the right and lists the suggested activities for the Task goal area

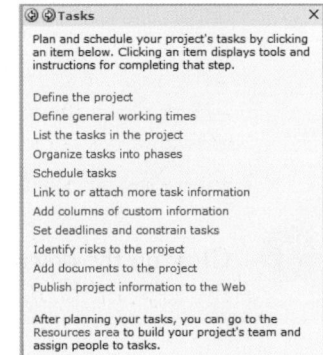

3 The main view area on the right-hand side displays the conventional project view (in the illustration below, the Gantt chart view is displayed)

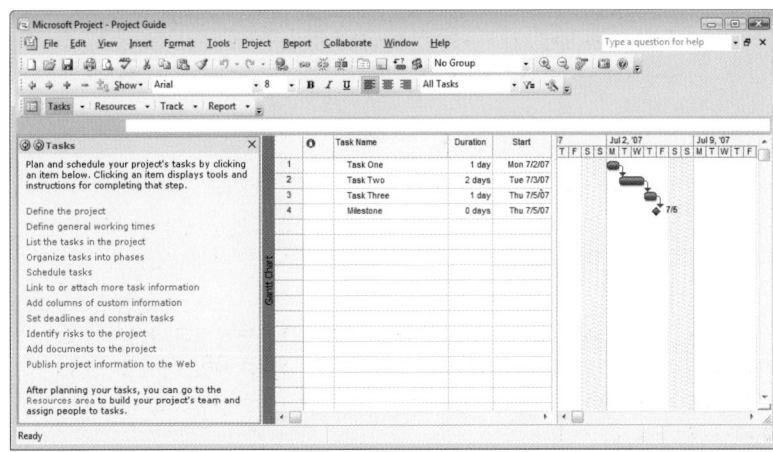

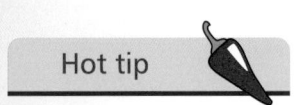

Hot tip

You can show or hide the Project Guide toolbar using View>Turn On/Turn Off Project Guide.

Tasks

The Tasks goal area will help you to set up your project and list the work to be done. It contains activities to set the start date; set up the project calendars; enter the tasks that will make up the project; structure the tasks into phases; schedule the tasks; attach notes; and set deadlines and constraints.

1. The Tasks goal area is normally displayed when you start a new project. If not, click the Tasks button on the Project Guide

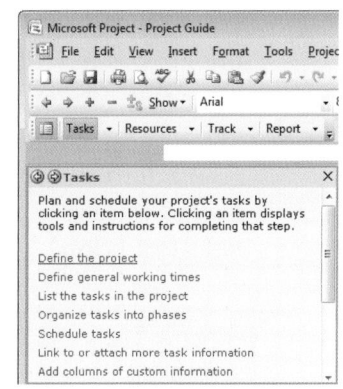

2. Click on Define the project in the side panel and Step 1 (Enter project information) will open in the side panel asking you to enter the start date for the project

3. Click on the down arrow to the right of the date field to select the start date from the drop down calendar (or type in the date) and click on Continue to Step 2

4. Select the default No to collaborate on the project (not illustrated) and click on Continue to Step 3

5. Click on Save and Finish and the side panel returns to the Tasks goal area to enable you to enter details

You can now enter further details about your project including defining working time and various other topics which are dealt with later in the book. The next topic will show you how to enter the project Tasks.

Beware

Working time can have a significant impact on your project schedule and is dealt with in detail in Project Calendars (chapter 9).

Listing the Tasks

The key activity in the Tasks goal area is Listing the tasks. The tasks represent the work activities that need to be carried out and they form the basic building blocks of your project.

1 Open the Project Guide, select the Tasks goal area and click on List the tasks in the project

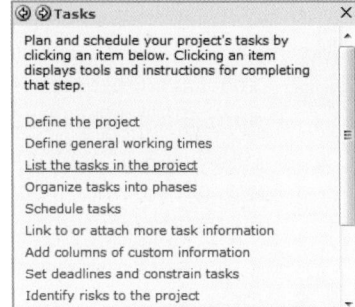

2 The side panel will now display instructions on how to enter your project tasks (see below)

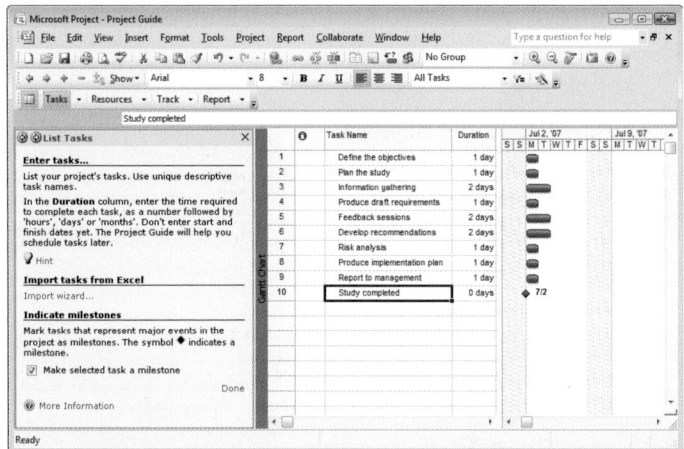

3 Click in the first Task Name field and type in the name of your first task, then click in the Duration field and enter the duration of the task (the default is days but you can also enter task duration in minutes, hours, weeks or months)

4 Carry on adding tasks and durations as above. To enter a project milestone type the milestone name in the Task Name field and select Make selected task a milestone

5 When you have finished listing your tasks click on Done at the bottom of the side panel

Resources

The Resources goal area allows you to define the people, and other resources, that will be used to carry out the tasks of the project. It contains activities to define the resources, set up calendars for resources, assign resources to tasks and add notes.

1 Open the project guide and select the Resources goal area

2 Click on Specify people and equipment for the project (underlined right) and you will be given options of selecting people from an address book, company server or entering them manually

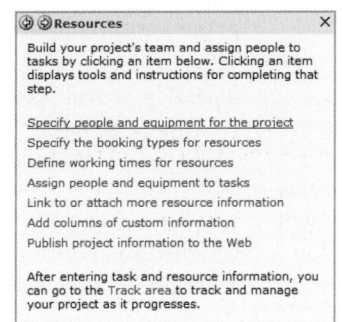

3 Select Enter resources manually and the detailed instructions for completing specifying the resources will be displayed in the side panel (see below)

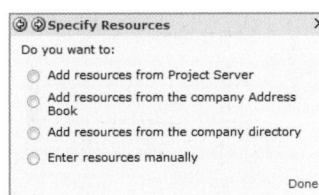

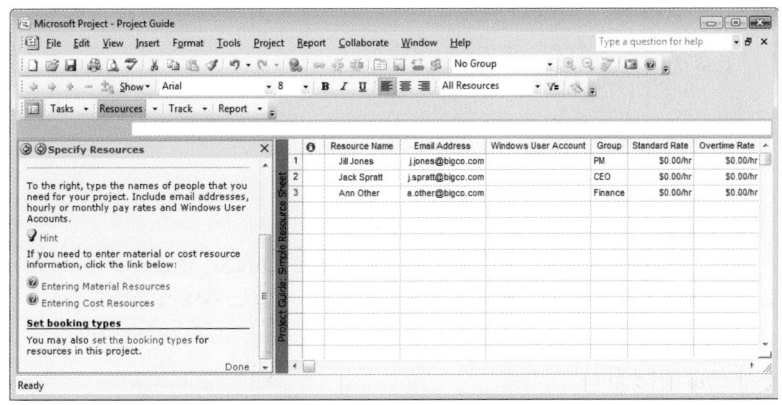

4 Type in the relevant details (as in the example above)

5 Once you have entered your resources click on Done at the bottom of the side panel

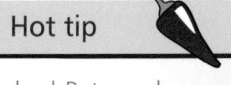

Hot tip

Standard Rate and Overtime Rate are dealt with in Project Costs (chapter 8).

Assign Resources

Having listed the tasks and defined the resources (people) who will work on them, the next step is to assign the resources to the tasks they will perform. This is done in the Resources goal area.

1 Open the project guide, select the Resource goal area, then click on Assign people and equipment to tasks and the side panel will display the Assign Resources details

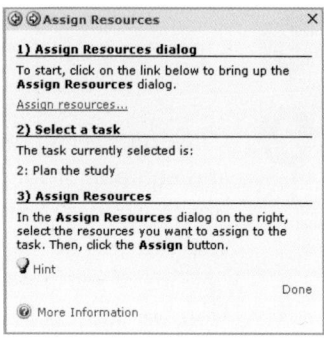

2 Click on Assign resources (underlined above right) which will open a separate Assign Resources dialog box (illustrated right)

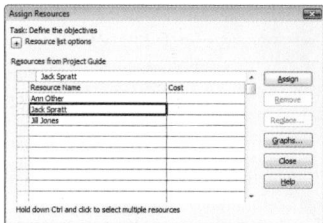

3 Select each task in turn in the Gantt chart (see below), then select the resource name (or names) you want to allocate to it in the Assign resource dialog box and click the Assign button

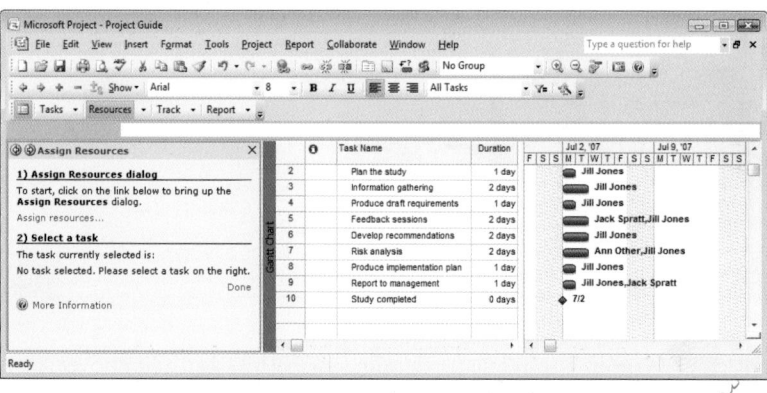

4 When all resource assignment is completed, click Close, then click Done at the bottom of the side panel

Linking Tasks

Having defined your tasks and assigned the people who will work on them, the next activity you may need to do in the project guide is to schedule the tasks. One of the simplest ways of scheduling tasks is to link them.

1 Open the project guide, select the Task goal area, then click on Schedule tasks and the side panel will display the Schedule Tasks details

2 Click on the first task name in the Gantt chart area, then hold down Ctrl and click on the next task (or the task you wish to link it to) so that they are both selected (see illustration below)

3 Now click on the first button in the side panel to create a Finish-to-Start link (this is the most common type of task dependency). The two tasks will be linked and scheduled so that the second task starts when the first is completed (as illustrated below)

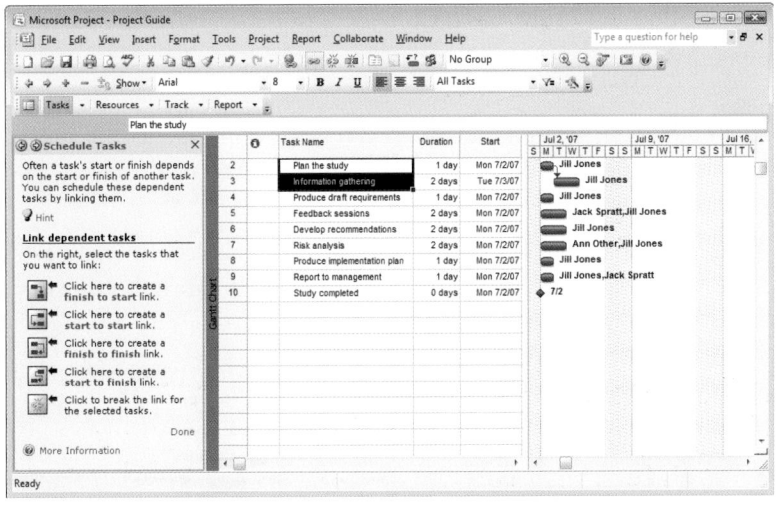

4 Carry on linking tasks by selecting the task you want to link from and then the task you want to link to

5 When all your tasks are linked click on Done at the bottom of the side panel

Track

Once your project is under way the Track goal area will help you to update the project with progress achieved.

1 Open project guide, select the Track goal area and click on Prepare to track the progress of your project in the side panel (underlined in the illustration below)

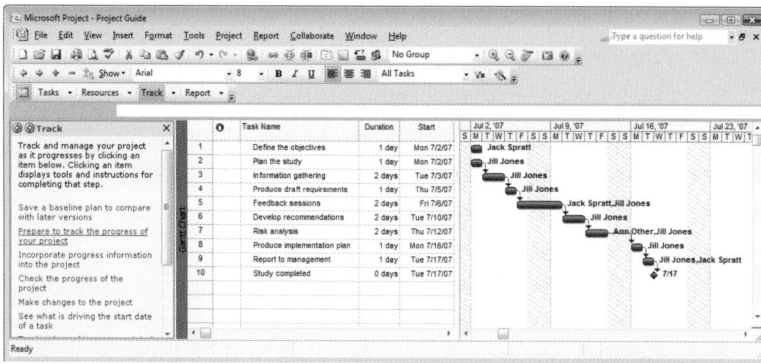

2 Setup tracking details appear in the side panel and you will be asked if you want your team to report progress through Project Server. Select No for manual tracking and click Continue

3 Select required method (Percentage complete is the most simple and recommended) and click Save and finish

4 Now enter the percent complete for each completed or part completed task directly into the % Work Complete field (as illustrated below)

	Task Name	Work	% Work Complete
1	Define the objectives	8 hrs	100%
2	Plan the study	8 hrs	75%
3	Information gathering	16 hrs	25%
4	Produce draft requirements	8 hrs	0%
5	Feedback sessions	32 hrs	0%
6	Develop recommendations	16 hrs	0%

5 When you have finished updating your tasks with the percentage complete, click on Check the progress of the project in the side panel to view the status

Report

In addition to tracking progress on your project, you will also want to view and report on it. View and reporting functionality is provided under the Report goal area.

1 Open project guide, select the Report goal area and click on Select a view or report in the side panel (underlined in the illustration right)

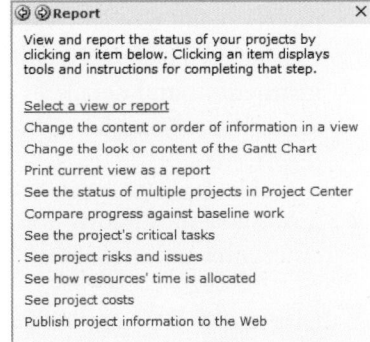

2 Select Create a project report and click on Display reports in the side panel to open the Reports dialog box (as illustrated right)

3 As an example, select Overview (as illustrated) and click on Select, a second Overview Reports dialog box will open, select Top-Level Tasks in this and again click on Select and the report will be produced in print preview (as below)

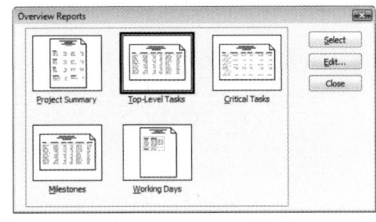

Top Level Tasks
Project Guide

ID	Task Name	Duration	Start	Finish	% Comp.	Cost	Work
1	Define the objectives	1 day	Mon 7/2/07	Mon 7/2/07	100%	$0.00	8 hrs
2	Plan the study	1 day	Tue 7/3/07	Tue 7/3/07	75%	$0.00	8 hrs
3	Information gathering	2 days	Wed 7/4/07	Thu 7/5/07	25%	$0.00	16 hrs
4	Produce draft requirements	1 day	Fri 7/6/07	Fri 7/6/07	0%	$0.00	8 hrs
5	Feedback sessions	2 days	Mon 7/9/07	Tue 7/10/07	0%	$0.00	32 hrs
6	Develop recommendations	2 days	Wed 7/11/07	Thu 7/12/07	0%	$0.00	16 hrs
7	Risk analysis	1 day	Fri 7/13/07	Fri 7/13/07	0%	$0.00	16 hrs
8	Produce implementation plan	1 day	Mon 7/16/07	Mon 7/16/07	0%	$0.00	8 hrs
9	Report to management	1 day	Tue 7/17/07	Tue 7/17/07	0%	$0.00	16 hrs
10	Study completed	0 days	Tue 7/17/07	Tue 7/17/07	0%	$0.00	0 hrs

4 Click on Print to print the report or Close to close it, then close the Reports dialog box and click on Done

Summary

- Project Guide provides a quick and easy way to start a new project using fairly basic (and somewhat limited) functionality

- Project Guide consists of three main components: the project guide toolbar (where you can select the Tasks, Resources, Track or Report goal areas); the side panel (where instructions and detailed choices are displayed); and the main view area (where the normal views, such as Gantt chart are displayed)

- Tasks goal area allows you to set up your project, set the start date, enter task details and schedule the tasks

- Listing the tasks is the option, within the Tasks goal area, where you enter the name and duration of each of the project tasks

- Resources goal area allows you to enter details of the people and any other resources you will use to carry out the project tasks

- Assign resources is the option, within the Resources goal area, where you can assign one or more people (or other resources) to each individual project task

- Schedule tasks is the option, within the Tasks goal area, which allows you to link tasks. The most common and straightforward way of linking tasks is in a finish-to-start dependency

- Track goal area is where you begin to track the progress of your project. The simplest way of entering details of the progress of each task is to enter the percentage complete

- Report goal area allows you to access the predefined reports and views available within Project

- The project guide provides a quick and simple way of carrying out these basic functions within Project. However, there are other ways of doing the same things, which also provide more detail and control. All of the functions covered in this chapter are described in more detail (with all the available options) later in this book

3 Managing your Project

This chapter introduces a structured approach to managing a project and explores some of the ways that Project 2007 can help you to manage your project.

A 4-Step Approach

Project management is the management of change.

In order to manage change, and therefore manage your project, you need to carry out a number of steps or tasks. But rather than just jumping straight in and defining these steps or tasks, it is a good idea to take a more structured approach to a project.

These four steps will give you just that:

1 Define the Objectives: start by identifying what you are trying to achieve, the project aims or goal, where you want to get to by the end of the project

2 Develop the Plan: once you have defined the objectives, then you can plan how you are going to go about achieving them

3 Carry it Out: once you have planned the project you need to carry it out or manage it until the project is completed and the objectives achieved

4 Hand it Over: once you have completed the project you have done your job as project manager

An awful lot of projects seem to start at Step 3! It's what's known as the "Just Do It" school of management. But even if you start your project at Step 2, what's the use of a plan if you don't know where you are going? So start by clearly identifying your goals.

Interestingly, the difficult step for some project managers is the last one. They find it difficult to let go.

The project manager's job is to implement change. Once that change has been implemented their role as a project manager is completed. The new, changed state becomes a production process and that requires production (rather than project) management.

In the remainder of this chapter we will expand on each of these four steps and look at what is involved, starting with Step 1, Defining the Objectives.

Beware

Experienced project managers may feel this is a simplistic approach. It is, but be patient as we will build on it in later sections.

Step 1: Define the Objectives

The first step in any project is to define the objectives. You need to do this in order to be able to:

- Make sure you have identified the right target

- Focus the other members of the project team on what the project is about

- Create team commitment to, and agreement about, the project objectives

- Ensure that you involve all interested parties in achieving a successful project outcome

When you set out to define your objectives, there is a useful acronym to remember: SMART. It stands for Strategic, Measurable, Agreed, Realistic, and Timed.

Strategic

The objectives must address some strategic business purpose or need. If they do not, does the project really matter to the business and, if not, why carry it out?

Measurable

If you can't measure project achievement, how will you know if you've achieved anything?

Agreed

If the rest of the business and the rest of the project team have not agreed with the objectives, there will be no commitment to achieving them.

Realistic

If the objectives are not realistic, the project team will soon realize that and lose any commitment to the project.

Timed

If there is no pressure to complete the project it will never get completed.

Note: some people use a different set of words for the SMART acronym (e.g. Specific, Measurable, Assignable or Achievable, Realistic and Time-related). It doesn't matter which words you use as long as they achieve a similar effect.

Hot tip

Define your project objectives now and make sure they are SMART.

Starting a Project

When you first start up Project 2007, it opens in Gantt chart view with a blank project file. The first thing you should do when creating a new project is to set the project start date.

1 Click on Project>Project Information from the menu bar to open the project information dialog box

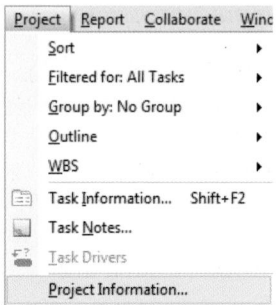

2 By default the start date will be the current date and you can change it by clicking the down arrow (to the right of the start date), which brings up a calendar from which you can select the required date (in the past or future)

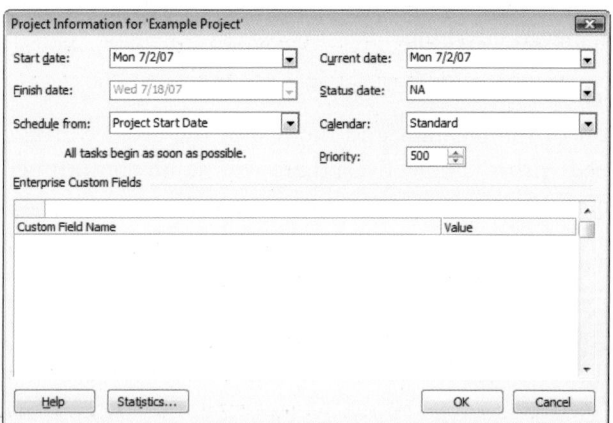

Beware

Scheduling back from a finish date is more difficult and should be avoided until you have some experience of forward-scheduling.

3 By default the project will be scheduled forward from the start date you select (note the finish date is not selectable). If required you can schedule a project backward by selecting Schedule from: Project finish date. This then makes the finish date active and the start date becomes deselected

Step 2: Develop the Plan

Having defined your project objectives, the next step is to plan how you will achieve them (or how you will get there), by developing the project plan.

Before we start developing the plan we need to look at some of the basic elements that make up a project plan. These are Tasks, Deliverables, Milestones and Resources:

Tasks

Tasks are the basic building blocks of the project. They represent the work that has to be carried out in order to complete the project. They will need to be carried out in some sort of sequence and they will also be interdependent with other tasks.

Deliverables

Deliverables (sometimes referred to as the products of a project) are the things that will be produced or delivered by the project along the way. Typically, they consist of progress or management reports, specifications of requirements, design documents and agreements, as well as the final result of the project (whatever that may be).

Hot tip

Deliverables provide the best way of measuring project progress.

Milestones

Milestones are the points during the project when you can accurately measure the progress of the project. They will typically be major events, such as agreement of requirements, approval of funding or final acceptance.

Resources

Resources are the people and other things (material and finance) that you will use on the project in order to carry out the tasks, produce the deliverables and meet the milestones.

To put these into the context of the project plan, the plan will set out the *Tasks* needed to produce the *Deliverables* and complete the project. It will also set out the *Resources* you will need to carry out the tasks and the *Milestones* you will use to measure your progress. The time line, or schedule, will set out when these things should happen.

The following topics will look at Tasks and Deliverables, Milestones and Resources in a bit more detail.

Tasks and Deliverables

Any project consists of a number of tasks which need to be completed. Depending on the project, it may consist of very few tasks or it may involve very many tasks. Some of these tasks will be relatively short tasks and others will take much longer to complete. Some will be critical to the success of the project, while others may be less important.

Having defined or clarified the objectives, the first step in producing your project plan is to begin listing the key tasks, these are the important ones, the ones that are critical to the success of the project. These will typically be related to a key deliverable. For example, if you were building a house, there would be a "design" task which would have the "house plans" as its deliverable.

If, for example, your project was a feasibility study, the key tasks and deliverables could be something like this:

Key Tasks	Deliverables
Define the objectives	Objectives
Plan the study	Project plan
Information gathering	Interview notes
Produce draft requirements	Draft requirements
Hold feedback sessions	Final requirements
Develop recommendations	Recommendations
Perform risk analysis	Risk log
Produce implementation plan	Implementation plan
Report to management	Final report

While you may well have many other tasks to carry out during your project, and may have other deliverables you need to produce, these should represent the major ones.

If you are not sure whether a task is a key task or not, play safe and include it. It is easy to remove something later if it is not required but missing something important at the start could be fatal to the project.

Hot tip

Although you should have already defined your objectives, it is still a good idea to include that task in your plan to record it.

Milestones

Project milestones are the events that mark the completion of a major task or group of tasks in a project.

Typical milestones would be the decision to proceed, selection of a supplier, acceptance of a major piece of work and, of course, completion of the project. Milestones often mark the acceptance of a key deliverable.

A milestone normally has a zero duration. In other words, it marks a single point in time when something happens. → deliverables

Once you have identified the key tasks and their deliverables in your project, you need to identify the major milestones. For a short project (such as a feasibility study) there may be only one milestone: completion of the study.

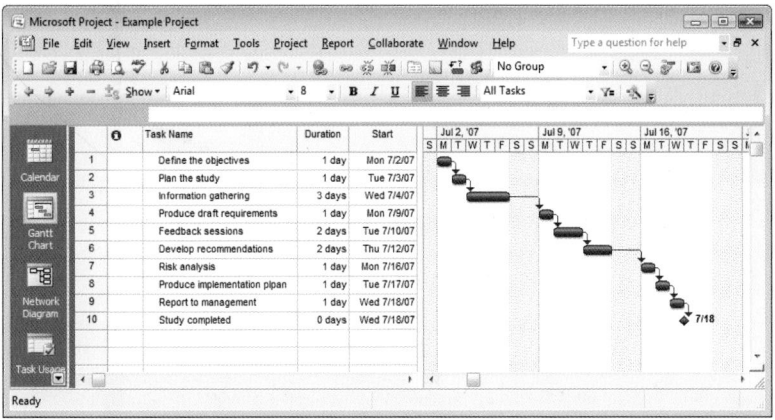

In the illustration above, the final task is a milestone, it has a zero duration and is indicated by a black diamond with the date on the right-hand side of the Gantt chart.

It is also possible to give a milestone a duration and still mark it as a milestone. This is covered in the next chapter.

For a longer project there may be more milestones, typically between three and eight. So once you have identified all your key tasks, take another look at your project and identify what you think your project milestones are.

In the next chapter we will look at how to enter and link tasks and milestones.

Resources

The key resources on most projects are the people who will work on the project. This will include the project manager and everyone else who will need to carry out any of the project's tasks. Resources are entered in the Resource Sheet.

1 Click on Resource Sheet in the View bar (it is near the bottom so you may need to scroll down to get to it) and the Resource sheet view will open in place of the Gantt chart

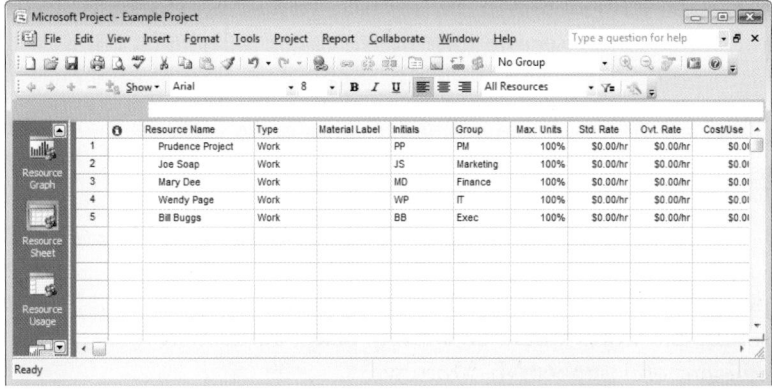

2 Type in the names, initials and groups for all the people who will be working on your project (including yourself of course). Leave the defaults in the other fields for now

3 If you need to add any material resources (we will deal with cost resources in a later chapter) to the project, enter their details and change the Type to Material

	ⓘ	Resource Name	Type	Material Label	Initials	Group	Max. Units
1		Prudence Project	Work		PP	PM	100%
2		Joe Soap	Work		JS	Marketing	100%
3		Mary Dee	Work		MD	Finance	100%
4		Wendy Page	Work		WP	IT	100%
5		Bill Buggs	Work		BB	Exec	100%
6		Paint	Material	gallon		Facilities	
7		Carpet	Material	square yard		Facilities	

Don't worry about the other columns in the resource sheet for now, they are covered in more detail in chapter 7 Resources.

Step 3: Carry it Out

If you've been through Step 1 (Define the Objectives) and Step 2 (Develop the Plan), then you know where you're going (the Objectives) and you know how you are going to get there (the Plan). On the basis of the plan and the required resources, you will also have received any business approval you need to continue, so you can now start carrying out the project.

There is often business pressure to skip these initial steps, particularly on smaller projects. It might sound good sense to just get stuck straight in and not waste time but it should be resisted. Carrying out a project without having clearly defined objectives and a proper plan has been compared to building a new type of bridge from A to B, without knowing exactly where A is and with the sure certainty that B will have moved by the time you get there.

Put simply, carrying out the project consists of allocating the necessary resources to the required tasks, tracking progress of the tasks until they are completed and measuring and reporting progress against your project milestones. If only life were that simple the world would be a lovely place, but along comes that eminent philosopher Mr Murphy:

> ## Murphy's First Law
>
> Whatever *can* go wrong,
> *will* go wrong

So you also need to expect problems and to plan how you will deal with them. If you don't your project could rapidly get knocked off course. One simple way of expecting problems is to build some contingency into the schedule and this is covered under the Contingency topic in chapter 5. There is a topic on Risk Management in chapter 8, which sets out a process for identifying and dealing with Risks (Murphy prevention).

Finally there is another benefit in expecting things to go wrong and it is known as the corollary to Murphy's First Law: "If you plan on it going wrong, it won't go wrong."

Saving Your Project

The chances are that, sooner or later, everyone who works with a computer will lose a large amount of work through a power cut or some other problem of outside their of control. I have even heard of some people (not me, of course) who caused the problem themselves!

So whenever you are working on a computer, save your work regularly. Project 2007 is no exception to this rule. By saving your work regularly you can try things out and will always be able to get back to where you saved. So save your project (and your sanity) by saving your work before (if you haven't already done so) and after making any major changes.

1. To save your file (replacing the previous version) simply click the Save button on the Toolbar or select File>Save from the Menu bar

2. If you want to preserve the previous version of the project select File>Save As from the Menu bar, select the directory where you want to save the file, give it a new file name and click Save

3. If you want to save the project file so that it can be opened in an earlier version of Project, use Save As and select the appropriate Type

4. If you click Save and the project file was created in an earlier version of Project, you will get a dialog box

5. Click Yes to save it in 2007 format or No to save in the original format. If you chose the latter, you will receive a further warning that features could be lost, click OK to continue with the save

Step 4: Hand it Over

Once the project is completed, the project manager's role is finished. However, some project managers have problems with this final step.

Letting Go

You have to let go and let the people who will be responsible for the ongoing operation take over managing the process. They won't like it or feel comfortable if the project manager is looking over their shoulders the whole time, so let them get on with it. You should have planned any required training for them and once they are up to speed, they will be fine.

Provide Support

But you cannot just drop a new process on the people who have to make it work and run! They will almost certainly have some problems adapting to new ways of doing things. What you must do is be available if they need you. This means scheduling some of your time to support the people carrying out the new process. This should only be for an initial, short, critical period (usually in the region of a month).

Finish the Paperwork

The hand over time is a great opportunity to finish off any outstanding paperwork or documentation. Tidy up the project files and back everything up.

Project Review

The last scheduled task on the project should be to arrange and hold a post-implementation review. This is the time when you can go back to the original objectives and see if they have been achieved or not. Was there anything that happened during the project that could not be dealt with or included in the project? If there was, should another project be initiated to deal with it?

As part of this review, the methods and tools used on the project should also be examined, and anything learned should be noted for the benefit of future projects.

Thank the Team

Last but not least, don't forget to thank everyone who helped you with the project, they will appreciate it. One of the nicest ways of thanking the project team is to take them out for a project team celebration meal.

Hot tip

Always invite your project sponsor and with any luck they will pick up the bill.

Summary

- Take a structured, 4-Step approach to project management: Define the objectives; Develop the plan; Carry it out; and Hand it over

- When defining your objectives it is good to check if they are SMART, that means Strategic, Measurable, Agreed, Realistic, and Timed

- When starting a project put in the start date before you start entering tasks and try to avoid scheduling back from a finish date

- Begin to develop your project plan by identifying the Tasks to be carried out, Deliverables that will be produced, the project Milestones and the Resources you will need to do it

- Try to identify all the key or important tasks and their associated deliverables at the outset

- Identify how many project milestones you will need and where they should go. They are entered just like tasks but with a zero duration

- Work out what people and other resources you will need on your project and enter them in the Resource Sheet view. If you don't know who they will be yet use a dummy name for the time being

- When carrying out the project, be aware that things will go wrong (Murphy's First Law) and plan for it with contingency and risk management

- Remember to save your project file regularly when you are making changes to it and save it back into an earlier format if you need to send it to someone with an earlier version of Project

- Handing the project over can sometimes be difficult but it has to be done. Use the project hand over to tidy things up and review how well the project went

- Finally don't forget to thank the people who helped on the project

4 Tasks and Milestones

Tasks represent the basic building blocks of a project and milestones are the reference points used to measure progress. This chapter will show the use of tasks and milestones to create the basic project plan.

Creating a Task

Tasks represent the basic building blocks of the project plan. They represent the pieces of work that will have to be done in order to carry out the project. Tasks can be entered in any view that includes a Task Name field, but the (default) Gantt Chart view is the easiest one in which to build up the task list.

1   Open a project file or create a new one and switch to Gantt chart view (if you are not already in it)

2   Click in the first Task Name field to select it

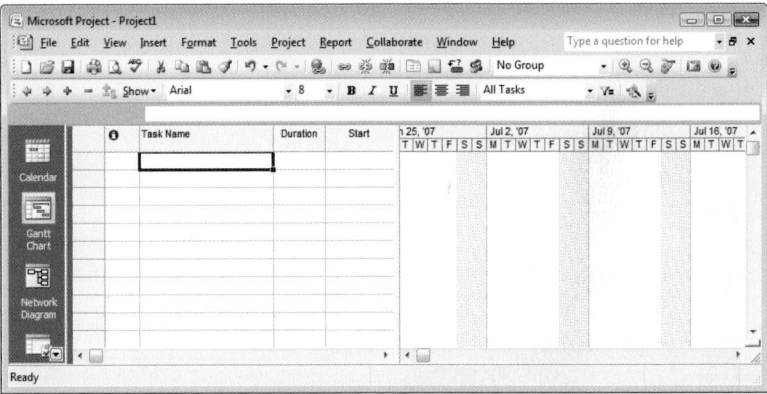

3   Type in the task name, e.g. Agree Project Objectives and press Enter

	🛈	Task Name	Duration	Start	Jul 2, '07
					S M T W T F S S
1		Agree Project Objectives	1 day?	Mon 7/2/07	

A Task ID (identity) of 1 is automatically assigned to the task (on the left-hand side above) and the default duration of 1 day is allocated. The question mark after the duration indicates that it is the default (estimated) duration. The task is scheduled to start on today's date (or the start date of the project if you have changed it) and a 1 day bar is shown on the Gantt chart to the right.

4   Click on the Save button (or select File>Save As from the Menu bar to name your project file and save it)

Hot tip

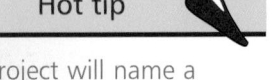

Project will name a new file Project 1 but it is worth naming it to something meaningful.

Task Duration

By default new tasks are created with an estimated duration of 1 day (indicated with a question mark after the duration). Once you enter a duration the question mark will be removed. You can change the duration by using the spin controls or by typing directly into the duration field.

Hot tip

You can put the question mark back if you wish by typing it after the duration.

1   Click on the Duration field and use the spin control (the up and down arrows that appear when the field is selected) to increase or reduce it

	ⓘ	Task Name	Duration	Start	Jul 2, '07 S M T W T F
1		Agree Project Objectives	2 days	Mon 7/2/07	

You can also click on the Duration field and just type in a number. It will default to the existing duration time type (days in this example).

2   To change the duration time type, you need to enter the number followed by m (minutes), h (hours), d (days), w (weeks) or mo (months)

	ⓘ	Task Name	Duration	Start	Jul 2, '07 S M T W T F
1		Agree Project Objectives	24 hrs	Mon 7/2/07	

3   In addition to working time (the default), you can also enter elapsed time by typing an "e" in front of the time type

	ⓘ	Task Name	Duration	Start	Jul 2, '07 S M T W T F
1		Agree Project Objectives	24 ehrs	Mon 7/2/07	

Note in the two illustrations above that 24 hours is scheduled to take three working days, while 24 elapsed hours takes just one day. This is because elapsed time includes all 24 hours in a day and all 7 days in a week, while working time only counts the working hours (8 by default) in a day and excludes weekends.

Adding Tasks

Additional tasks can be added to a project at any time. The tasks can be added after existing tasks or inserted in between or in front of existing tasks. We will look at doing both.

1 To add new tasks to the end, click on the first blank Task Name field and type in your new task name, press the tab key, type in the duration and press Enter

	❶	Task Name	Duration	Start	Jul 2, '07 S M T W T F S
1		Agree Project Objectives	1 day	Mon 7/2/07	
2		Select Project Team	2 days	Mon 7/2/07	

2 To insert a task into an existing task list, click on the task name that you want to insert the new task in front of and select Insert>New Task from the menu bar

	❶	Task Name	Duration	Start	Jul 2, '07 S M T W T F S
1		Agree Project Objectives	1 day	Mon 7/2/07	
2					
3		Select Project Team	2 days	Mon 7/2/07	
4		Produce Outline Project Plan	1 day	Mon 7/2/07	
5		Identify Business Case	2 days	Mon 7/2/07	
6		Analyze the Risks	1 day	Mon 7/2/07	

3 Then type in the new task name, then tab to the duration field and enter the duration

	❶	Task Name	Duration	Start	Jul 2, '07 S M T W T F S
1		Agree Project Objectives	1 day	Mon 7/2/07	
2		Identify Stakeholders	1 day	Mon 7/2/07	
3		Select Project Team	2 days	Mon 7/2/07	
4		Produce Outline Project Plan	1 day	Mon 7/2/07	
5		Identify Business Case	2 days	Mon 7/2/07	
6		Analyze the Risks	1 day	Mon 7/2/07	

Continue to add tasks as necessary to build up your task list. At the moment they are all scheduled to start immediately and run concurrently, the next two topics will address this.

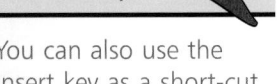

Hot tip

You can also use the Insert key as a short-cut to insert a new task.

Hot tip

If a task name does not quite fit in the field, double-click the Task Name column header and select Best Fit.

Task Dependencies

Tasks do not exist in isolation, most will be dependant on one or more other tasks and they will have one or more other tasks dependant on them. The only exceptions to this are the first and last task in the project.

In the following illustration, task 2 requires something from and is therefore dependant on task 1 being completed before it can begin. In a similar way task 3 is dependant on task 2.

In Project 2007 you create these dependencies by linking the appropriate tasks. Linking tasks allows you to specify the circumstances where the start or finish of a task is dependant on the start or finish of another task or tasks.

Finish-to-start

The most common type of dependency or link is the finish-to-start dependency (as illustrated above) where the finish of task 1 allows task 2 to start. Typically this is where task 2 needs something that is produced in task 1. On the Gantt chart the link is shown as on the right.

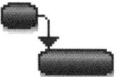

There are three other types of links:

Start-to-start

This is where task 2 can start as soon as task 1 starts and can take place at the same time. It is shown on the Gantt chart as on the right.

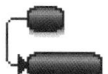

Finish-to-finish

This is used where task 2 has to finish at the same time as task 1 and is shown as on the right.

Start-to-finish

In this case when task 1 starts task 2 must finish and is shown as on the right.

These three (and particularly the last one) are likely to be the exception rather than the rule.

Beware

It is best to avoid the start-to-finish link if possible as it can cause some problems.

Linking Tasks

Task dependencies are created by linking tasks. The default dependency is the finish-to-start dependency and this will normally be the way you will want to link most of the tasks in your project. The quickest approach is to link all the tasks in this way to start with and then make any required changes.

1 Click on the Task Name column header to select all your task names

Hot tip

You can also select several tasks by dragging across the task names or task IDs.

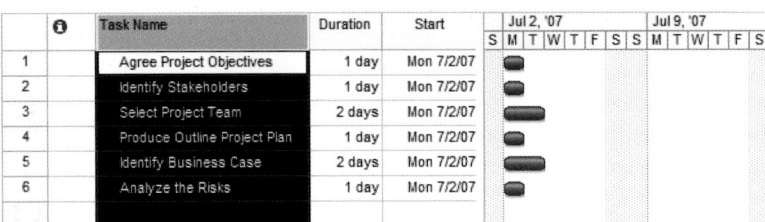

	ⓘ	Task Name	Duration	Start	Jul 2, '07							Jul 9, '07						
					S	M	T	W	T	F	S	S	M	T	W	T	F	S
1		Agree Project Objectives	1 day	Mon 7/2/07														
2		Identify Stakeholders	1 day	Mon 7/2/07														
3		Select Project Team	2 days	Mon 7/2/07														
4		Produce Outline Project Plan	1 day	Mon 7/2/07														
5		Identify Business Case	2 days	Mon 7/2/07														
6		Analyze the Risks	1 day	Mon 7/2/07														

2 Click the Link tasks button (shown on the right) on the toolbar

	ⓘ	Task Name	Duration	Start	Jul 2, '07							Jul 9, '07						
					S	M	T	W	T	F	S	S	M	T	W	T	F	S
1		Agree Project Objectives	1 day	Mon 7/2/07														
2		Identify Stakeholders	1 day	Tue 7/3/07														
3		Select Project Team	2 days	Wed 7/4/07														
4		Produce Outline Project Plan	1 day	Fri 7/6/07														
5		Identify Business Case	2 days	Mon 7/9/07														
6		Analyze the Risks	1 day	Wed 7/11/07														

The tasks are all linked in a finish-to-start dependency.

You can also link tasks by holding down the Ctrl key, clicking the individual task names and then clicking the Link tasks button.

Links are always created in the direction in which you select the tasks. Selecting task 2 and then task 1 will result in a link from task 2 to task 1. Task 1 will then be dependent on task 2.

3 If you are happy with the way your tasks are linked, save your project file before you start changing anything else

Try to get into the habit of saving your project file each time you make a change, you will be very glad you did one day.

Unlinking Tasks

Having linked all the tasks in the project in a finish-to-start dependency you may need to unlink some.

1 Select the two tasks you wish to unlink (hold down the Ctrl key and click on the two task names)

	ⓘ	Task Name	Duration	Start	Jul 2, '07	Jul 9, '07
					S M T W T F S	S M T W T F S
1		Agree Project Objectives	1 day	Mon 7/2/07		
2		Identify Stakeholders	1 day	Tue 7/3/07		
3		Select Project Team	2 days	Wed 7/4/07		
4		Produce Outline Project Plan	1 day	Fri 7/6/07		
5		Identify Business Case	2 days	Mon 7/9/07		
6		Analyze the Risks	1 day	Wed 7/11/07		

2 Click the Unlink button on the toolbar and the link is removed

	ⓘ	Task Name	Duration	Start	Jul 2, '07	Jul !
					S M T W T F S	S M
1		Agree Project Objectives	1 day	Mon 7/2/07		
2		Identify Stakeholders	1 day	Tue 7/3/07		
3		Select Project Team	2 days	Mon 7/2/07		
4		Produce Outline Project Plan	1 day	Wed 7/4/07		
5		Identify Business Case	2 days	Thu 7/5/07		
6		Analyze the Risks	1 day	Mon 7/9/07		

3 An alternative way of accessing the link between tasks is to double-click on the link line between the two tasks you wish to unlink on the Gantt chart. This will open the Task Dependency dialog box

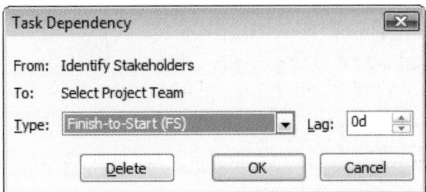

4 Click Delete and the link is removed

You can also unlink several tasks at the same time by selecting them all and then clicking the Unlink button.

Changing Dependencies

Although the majority of tasks in a project will normally be in a finish-to-start dependency, you will sometimes need to change the dependency to one of the other types.

1 Re-establish any dependency you removed in the previous exercise by selecting the tasks and clicking the Link button on the toolbar

2 Double-click on the link between the tasks, where you wish to change the dependency, to bring up the Task Dependency dialog box

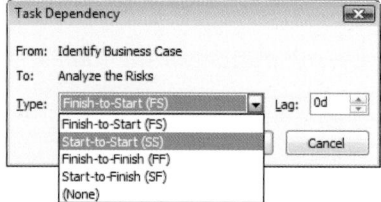

3 Click on the down arrow to the right of Type to bring up the drop-down list of options (as above)

4 Select Start-to-Start (SS), the second option, click OK and the two tasks will be rescheduled to start on the same day (as below)

	🛈	Task Name	Duration	Start	Jul 2, '07 S M T W T F S	Jul 9, '07 S M T W T F S
1		Agree Project Objectives	1 day	Mon 7/2/07		
2		Identify Stakeholders	1 day	Tue 7/3/07		
3		Select Project Team	2 days	Wed 7/4/07		
4		Produce Outline Project Plan	1 day	Fri 7/6/07		
5		Identify Business Case	2 days	Mon 7/9/07		
6		Analyze the Risks	1 day	Mon 7/9/07		

The four types of dependency were defined on page 47 (Task Dependencies). Selecting (None) on the drop-down list of options removes the dependency and therefore is another way of unlinking tasks.

If you are working through these exercises, save your project file before you carry on with the remainder of this topic.

We will now look at creating a finish-to-finish dependency and a start-to-finish dependency.

5 Double-click on the link between the tasks you wish to change to bring up the Task Dependency dialog box

6 Select Finish-to-Finish as the dependency type, click OK and the two tasks will be rescheduled so that the second task finishes on the same day as the first task

	ⓘ	Task Name	Duration	Start	Jul 2, '07 S M T W T F S
1		Agree Project Objectives	1 day	Mon 7/2/07	
2		Identify Stakeholders	1 day	Tue 7/3/07	
3		Select Project Team	2 days	Mon 7/2/07	
4		Produce Outline Project Plan	1 day	Wed 7/4/07	
5		Identify Business Case	2 days	Thu 7/5/07	
6		Analyze the Risks	1 day	Thu 7/5/07	

In the illustration above, task 3 has been put in a finish-to-finish dependency to task 2. As it has a duration of 2 days it has now been rescheduled to start one day ahead of task 2 so that it can finish at the same time.

Now let us see what happens when we change a dependency to start-to-finish.

7 Select the tasks you wish to change (in the following example we are using tasks 4 and 5), change the dependency to Start-to-Finish and click OK

	ⓘ	Task Name	Duration	Start	Jul 2, '07 S M T W T F S
1		Agree Project Objectives	1 day	Mon 7/2/07	
2		Identify Stakeholders	1 day	Tue 7/3/07	
3		Select Project Team	2 days	Mon 7/2/07	
4		Produce Outline Project Plan	1 day	Wed 7/4/07	
5		Identify Business Case	2 days	Mon 7/2/07	
6		Analyze the Risks	1 day	Mon 7/2/07	

Project has now rescheduled task 5 so that it finishes when task 4 starts. This is a fairly clumsy type of dependency to use and a better alternative may often be to change the two tasks around.

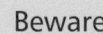

Beware

If you are doing the exercises in each topic, do not save your project at this point, use the one you saved after step 4.

Moving a Task

If you wish to move a task to a new position in the task list, the easiest way is to use drag-and-drop. Select the ID of the task (or tasks) that you want to move and drag them to their new position.

1 Click once on the Task ID of the task you want to move to select the whole task and release the mouse button

	ⓘ	Task Name	Duration	Start	Jul 2, '07	Jul 9, '07
					S M T W T F S	S M T W T F S
1		Agree Project Objectives	1 day	Mon 7/2/07		
2		Identify Stakeholders	1 day	Tue 7/3/07		
3		Select Project Team	2 days	Wed 7/4/07		
4		Produce Outline Project Plan	1 day	Fri 7/6/07		
5		Identify Business Case	2 days	Mon 7/9/07		
6		Analyze the Risks	1 day	Mon 7/9/07		

2 Now click on the task ID again but this time do not release the mouse button and drag the task up or down the task list as required. Notice the insertion point marker (see shaded line above) as you drag

3 When you get to the desired new location release the mouse button

	ⓘ	Task Name	Duration	Start	Jul 2, '07	Jul 9, '07
					S M T W T F S	S M T W T F S
1		Agree Project Objectives	1 day	Mon 7/2/07		
2		Identify Stakeholders	1 day	Tue 7/3/07		
3		Select Project Team	2 days	Wed 7/4/07		
4		Identify Business Case	2 days	Fri 7/6/07		
5		Analyze the Risks	1 day	Fri 7/6/07		
6		Produce Outline Project Plan	1 day	Mon 7/2/07		

The task is moved to its new location and, in the example above, the links have been removed. Links are generally removed if a task is dragged to the start or end of a task list (as in this example), but if not you may wish to delete them if they are no longer appropriate.

4 To relink the task in its new position (in the example above), you could establish a link from task 4 to task 6 and another link from task 5 to task 6 (see the first screen shot in the next topic for how this should look)

Deleting a Task

If you need to delete a task from a task list, simply select it and delete it.

1 Select the task to be deleted by clicking on its Task ID

	ⓘ	Task Name	Duration	Start	Jul 2, '07	Jul 9, '07
					S M T W T F S	S M T W T F S
1		Agree Project Objectives	1 day	Mon 7/2/07		
2		Identify Stakeholders	1 day	Tue 7/3/07		
3		Select Project Team	2 days	Wed 7/4/07		
4		Identify Business Case	2 days	Fri 7/6/07		
5		Analyze the Risks	1 day	Fri 7/6/07		
6		Produce Outline Project Plan	1 day	Tue 7/10/07		

2 Then click Edit>Delete Task on the menu bar and the task is removed from the project

	ⓘ	Task Name	Duration	Start	Jul 2, '07	Jul 9, '07
					S M T W T F S	S M T W T F S
1		Agree Project Objectives	1 day	Mon 7/2/07		
2		Select Project Team	2 days	Tue 7/3/07		
3		Identify Business Case	2 days	Thu 7/5/07		
4		Analyze the Risks	1 day	Thu 7/5/07		
5		Produce Outline Project Plan	1 day	Mon 7/9/07		

3 If you delete the wrong task (or tasks) in error you can reverse your previous actions using the Undo button on the toolbar

4 You can also delete individual fields or whole tasks by selecting the Task name and pressing the Delete key. This will bring up a smart tag asking you to confirm what you want to delete (see below)

4		Identify Business Case	2 days	Fri 7/6/07
5	✕ ▾		1 day	Fri 7/6/07
6				e 7/10/07
	⊙	Only clear the contents of Task Name Cell.		
	○	Delete the entire task.		

5 Click on Only clear the contents of the selected cell and the task name will be deleted or click on Delete the entire task and the whole task will be deleted

If you make a mistake you can always use the Undo button.

Beware

In Project 2007 you can undo a series of steps, in earlier versions of Project you can only undo one step!

Beware

Versions of Project before 2002 do not have Smart Tags.

Task Form

Task Entry view (which brings up the Task Form) is one of the additional views that is available in Project. It is used to enter, view and edit details of individual tasks.

1 Scroll down the View Bar (on the left-hand side of the Project screen) until More Views appears

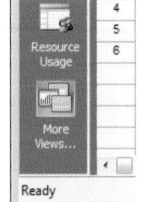

2 Click the More Views button and the More Views dialog box opens

3 Scroll down through the More Views list, select Task Entry, click Apply and the Task Form is displayed in the lower half of the screen (as illustrated in the example below)

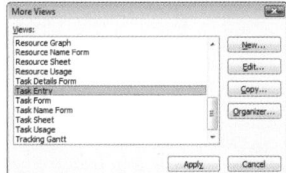

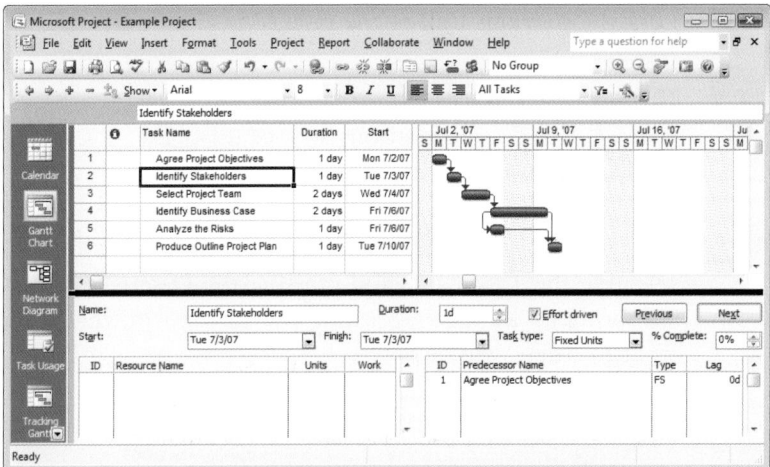

4 You can now view, enter and edit task details directly in the lower pane

5 The split bar (shown in black in the illustration above) can be moved up or down as required and double-clicking on it will hide the Task Form and return to the basic Gantt chart view

Project Milestones

Project milestones represent the significant events that mark the progress of a project. The most straightforward way of inserting a project milestone is to enter a task with a zero duration.

1 Select a blank task at the end of your project (or press Insert anywhere in the task list) to insert a milestone

	❶	Task Name	Duration	Start	Jul 2, '07							Jul 9, '07					
					S	M	T	W	T	F	S	S	M	T	W	T	F	S
1		Agree Project Objectives	1 day	Mon 7/2/07													
2		Identify Stakeholders	1 day	Tue 7/3/07													
3		Select Project Team	2 days	Wed 7/4/07													
4		Identify Business Case	2 days	Fri 7/6/07													
5		Analyze the Risks	1 day	Fri 7/6/07													
6		Produce Outline Project Plan	1 day	Tue 7/10/07													

2 Type the milestone name, tab across to the Duration field, type "0" (zero), press Enter and a milestone is inserted

3 Link the previous task to the milestone

	❶	Task Name	Duration	Start	Jul 2, '07							Jul 9, '07					
					S	M	T	W	T	F	S	S	M	T	W	T	F	S
1		Agree Project Objectives	1 day	Mon 7/2/07													
2		Identify Stakeholders	1 day	Tue 7/3/07													
3		Select Project Team	2 days	Wed 7/4/07													
4		Identify Business Case	2 days	Fri 7/6/07													
5		Analyze the Risks	1 day	Fri 7/6/07													
6		Produce Outline Project Plan	1 day	Tue 7/10/07													
7		Project Approval	0 days	Tue 7/10/07											◆ 7/10		

4 To add a duration to the milestone click in the Duration field and enter a duration, then double-click the milestone task name to open the Task Information dialog box

5 Click the Advanced tab, check Mark Task as Milestone (bottom left) and click OK

	❶	Task Name	Duration	Start	Jul 2, '07							Jul 9, '07						Jul 16, '07				
					S	M	T	W	T	F	S	S	M	T	W	T	F	S	S	M	T	W	T	F	S
1		Agree Project Objectives	1 day	Mon 7/2/07																		
2		Identify Stakeholders	1 day	Tue 7/3/07																		
3		Select Project Team	2 days	Wed 7/4/07																		
4		Identify Business Case	2 days	Fri 7/6/07																		
5		Analyze the Risks	1 day	Fri 7/6/07																		
6		Produce Outline Project Plan	1 day	Tue 7/10/07																		
7		Project Approval	5 days	Wed 7/11/07															◆ 7/17		

Beware

In versions of Project before 2007, milestone duration did not show on the link line in the Gantt chart.

Recurring Tasks

Any task that is regularly repeated in a project is called a recurring task. It could be a project team meeting, a meeting with your project sponsor or the production of a monthly report.

The procedure for setting up a recurring task is different from creating a normal task and you cannot convert a normal task into a recurring task.

1 To insert a recurring task, click in an empty Task Name field, then select Insert>Recurring Task from the menu bar and the Recurring Task Information dialog box will appear

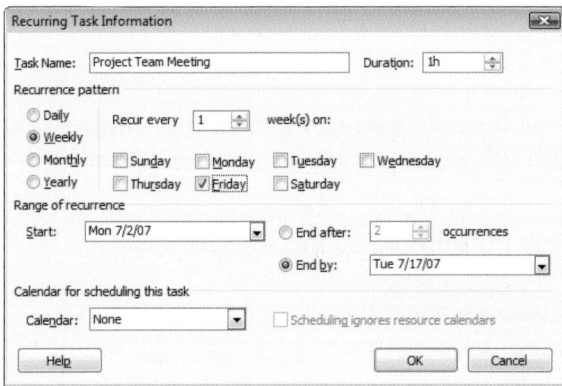

2 Enter the task name, duration, recurrence and range information (as in the above example) and click OK

	ⓘ	Task Name	Duration	Start	Jul 2, '07	Jul 9, '07	Jul 16, '07
					S M T W T F S	S M T W T F S	S M T W T F S
1		Agree Project Objectives	1 day	Mon 7/2/07			
2		Identify Stakeholders	1 day	Tue 7/3/07			
3		Select Project Team	2 days	Wed 7/4/07			
4	.	Identify Business Case	2 days	Fri 7/6/07			
5		Analyze the Risks	1 day	Fri 7/6/07			
6		Produce Outline Project Plan	1 day	Tue 7/10/07			
7		Project Approval	5 days	Wed 7/11/07			7/17
8							
9	↻	+ Project Team Meeting	5.13 days	Fri 7/6/07			

The recurring task is inserted into the task list. The "+" next to the task name indicates it consists of a number of subtasks (two in this case, one for each meeting). Clicking on the "+" will display the individual meetings. Double-clicking the task name will bring up the Recurring Task Information dialog box and allow editing.

Work Effort v Duration

One of the principal reasons for breaking a project down into tasks is that it is far easier to plan, allocate and control smaller packets of work. This topic is concerned with the process of estimating how much work a task will require (the work effort) and how long it will take to complete that work (the duration). Be warned the two are very rarely the same.

Work Effort

When it comes to estimating how much work will be involved in a task you can base it on one (or a combination) of four options:

- Experience: if you have done a similar task before, you can base it on how much work effort that required

- Advice: if you know someone who has done something similar, you can ask them how much work it involved

- Guidelines: your organization or industry may have guidelines for estimating that you can use

- Guess: if none of the other options are available to you, then your guess is probably as good as anyone else's

So that gives you an initial estimate of how much work is involved in the task, but how long will it actually take the person who is going to do it?

Duration

Microsoft Project basically treats work effort and duration in a fairly simplistic way. If you double the resources on a task it will halve the duration. It does not usually work like that in real life.

Duration will be dependant on the amount of time the person carrying out the task has available and what other work they have to do at the same time. If they are allocated to your project 100% of the time there will be fewer problems but that is rarely the case.

The most effective way is to ask the person who will be doing it how long it will take them. But in the early stages of planning a project you won't always know who will be doing the work. In the absence of anything else a factor of 50% would be sensible, so if it looks like about 4 days work effort you should set the duration to 6 days assuming one person will do it.

Don't forget

The person most likely to know how long a task will take is the person who will be doing it.

Summary

- Tasks are the basic building blocks of a project plan, they are best entered in Gantt chart view and a task is created by typing the task name in a blank Task name field

- Task duration can be defined in minutes, hours, days, weeks or even months. It can be typed in or set using the spinner controls

- Tasks can be added to the end of a task list or they can be inserted using Insert>New Task (or the Insert key); they will be inserted in front of the selected task

- There are four types of task dependency: finish-to-start is the most common dependency, but tasks can also be linked in finish-to-finish, start-to-start or start-to-finish

- Tasks are linked to form dependencies using the link task button and can also be unlinked using the unlink task button

- Task dependencies can be changed or deleted by double-clicking on the link line between the tasks

- Tasks can be moved up or down the task list by selecting the task and dragging it up or down to its new place. You may need to re-establish any links after this move

- Tasks can be deleted using Edit>Delete Task from the menu bar or using the Delete key and smart tag

- The undo button can reverse any mistakes you may make but it is safest to save your project file regularly

- The task form can be applied to the Gantt chart to give more detail and control over a task

- Project milestones are created as tasks with zero duration or they can be set through the task information dialog box

- Recurring tasks need to be set up using Insert>Recurring Task from the menu bar. They can then be edited by double-clicking the task name

- When estimating task duration it is important to remember that the duration is very rarely the same as the work effort

5 Adding Structure

In this chapter, we start to add some structure to the project by developing summary tasks and subtasks and using outlining.

Project Structure

A simple project, such as carrying out a feasibility study, might consist of no more than 10 or 12 tasks. A medium-sized project, such as introducing a new business venture or planning and organizing an exhibition, could run into over one hundred individual tasks. While a very large project, such as building a new airport, could run into many thousands of tasks.

Work Breakdown Structure

If you try to identify and plan every single task in your project right from the start, you will almost certainly be doomed to failure. In the early stages of a project there are just too many uncertainties and unknown factors, which will only become known as the project progresses. To cope with this a project needs to be broken down into manageable chunks, one level at a time. This is known as the Work Breakdown Structure (WBS).

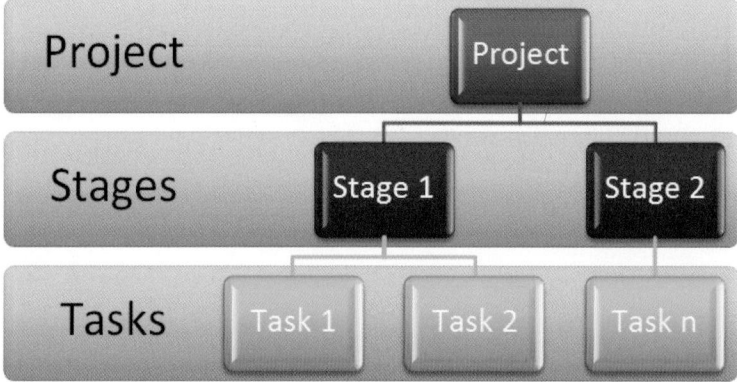

1   First break your project down into discrete chunks, with their own deliverables, these are usually referred to as Stages (but they may also be called Phases)

2   Then in turn, break each Stage into the Tasks that will be needed to carry it out

3   Finally each Task may also need to be broken down into one (or more) levels of Subtasks (not shown in the diagram above), depending on the size of the project and the size of the task

Summary Tasks

In Microsoft Project, structure is implemented through Subtasks and Summary Tasks. Any task that has a subtask is itself a summary task. Therefore a task can be a subtask of another task and a summary task itself. Project Stages are summary tasks.

A summary task is created in exactly the same way as any other task but its subtasks are indented.

1 Click on the Task Name of the task in front of which you want to create a summary task and press the Insert key

2 Type in the name for the summary task (in this example Stage 1) and press Enter. Notice, in the example below, that it is inserted as a task, with a default duration of 1 day. We still need to make it a summary task

	❶	Task Name	Duration	Start	Jul 2, '07	Jul 9, '07	Jul 16, '07
					S M T W T F S	S M T W T F S	S M T W T F S
1		Stage 1	1 day?	Mon 7/2/07			
2		Agree Project Objectives	1 day	Mon 7/2/07			
3		Identify Stakeholders	1 day	Tue 7/3/07			
4		Select Project Team	2 days	Wed 7/4/07			
5		Identify Business Case	2 days	Fri 7/6/07			
6		Analyze the Risks	1 day	Fri 7/6/07			
7		Produce Outline Project Plan	1 day	Tue 7/10/07			
8		Project Approval	5 days	Wed 7/11/07			7/17

3 Select all the tasks you want to be subtasks to this summary task by dragging across the task names and click the Indent button

	❶	Task Name	Duration	Start	Jul 2, '07	Jul 9, '07	Jul 16, '07
					S M T W T F S	S M T W T F S	S M T W T F S
1		− Stage 1	12 days	Mon 7/2/07			
2		Agree Project Objectives	1 day	Mon 7/2/07			
3		Identify Stakeholders	1 day	Tue 7/3/07			
4		Select Project Team	2 days	Wed 7/4/07			
5		Identify Business Case	2 days	Fri 7/6/07			
6		Analyze the Risks	1 day	Fri 7/6/07			
7		Produce Outline Project Pla	1 day	Tue 7/10/07			
8		Project Approval	5 days	Wed 7/11/07			7/17

The indented tasks have all now been indented to the right and have become subtasks of the inserted summary task. The summary task is now shown in bold with a black summary bar on the Gantt chart. The duration of the summary task has been set to the duration of all its subtasks. Note in the example above the subtasks add up to 13 days but Task 6 is concurrent with Task 5 so the summary task correctly shows 12 days duration.

Don't forget

You can also select multiple tasks by holding down the Ctrl key and clicking on each task.

Project Stages

Conventionally in project management methodology, the first-level summary tasks are referred to as project stages.

Project management methodology initially grew out of the construction industry and still retains some of that industry's terminology. In later years it has also been influenced by the information technology industry which, interestingly, has a lot of similarities.

Using that influence, we can now build a little further on our 4-step approach by expanding our second step (plan how we will get there) into two separate stages. The first is to determine what the detailed business needs are and the second is to define what we will need to do to achieve those needs.

If this sounds a bit like "overkill", keep an open mind for the time being. Hopefully, as we develop the process further, you will begin to see why this is a useful approach. These five project stages are conventionally referred to as:

Initiation
To define the project objectives and the team structure, produce the initial (outline) project plan and get the project started.

Strategy
To determine what the detailed business needs are and what the potential payback will be when we achieve them.

Analysis
To define what will need to be done in order to meet the business needs.

Design and Build
Carrying out the project by doing the detailed design of how it will be done and then doing it (i.e. build it, buy it, etc.).

Implementation
To install and hand over the new process and close the project.

The chief benefit of this approach is that the major expense or effort usually occurs in the Design and Build stage. At each of the preceding stages the potential investment and benefits can be reappraised to ensure that it will still be viable. If not the project can be wound up with minimal cost to the business.

Hot tip

There is nothing sacred about these five stages or their names. They are just a suggested starting point and they should be adapted to suit your own project.

While a five stage approach may be superfluous for a feasibility study, most small- to medium-sized projects will usually have between three and eight project stages. Use whichever of the five stages are appropriate to your project and add any further stages you feel the project needs.

Adding Project Stages

Having decided on the number of stages, you can initially add them to the project with a dummy task under each. These can be replaced later, when you have identified the real tasks.

1. If you have not already created the first project stage in the Summary Task topic (page 61) do it now

2. Click on the first blank Task Name field after your first stage and type in your other project stages with a dummy task plus duration (e.g. 20 days) after each stage

	❶	Task Name	Duration	Start	Jul 2, '07	Jul 9, '07	Jul 16, '07	Jul 23, '07
					S M T W T F S	S M T W T F S	S M T W T F S	S M T W T F S
1		− Initiation Stage	20 days?	Mon 7/2/07				
2		Agree Project Objectives	1 day	Mon 7/2/07				
3		Identify Stakeholders	1 day	Tue 7/3/07				
4		Select Project Team	2 days	Wed 7/4/07				
5		Identify Business Case	2 days	Fri 7/6/07				
6		Analyze the Risks	1 day	Fri 7/6/07				
7		Produce Outline Project Plan	1 day	Tue 7/10/07				
8		Project Approval	5 days	Wed 7/11/07			7/17	
9		Strategy Stage	1 day?	Mon 7/2/07				
10		Dummy Task	20 days	Mon 7/2/07				
11		Analysis Stage	1 day?	Mon 7/2/07				
12		Dummy Task	20 days	Mon 7/2/07				
13		Design & Build Stage	1 day?	Mon 7/2/07				
14		Dummy Task	20 days	Mon 7/2/07				
15		Implementation Stage	1 day?	Mon 7/2/07				
16		Dummy Task	20 days	Mon 7/2/07				

Don't forget

If your task names don't fit, double-click the Task Name column header and select Best Fit.

Notice that the stages and dummy tasks have all been inserted as subtasks of the first stage. We need to use the Outdent button to make the other stages summary tasks. We will also need to link the new tasks.

3. Click on each stage name and click the Outdent button to make the stages summary tasks

4. Finally link the last task in the first stage to the first task in the second stage and so on, so that all the tasks in the project are linked (your project should then look like the first illustration on the following page)

Changing the Timescale

Once you begin to link all the tasks in a project, they will quickly vanish off the timescale in the right-hand pane and you won't be able to see the whole project. This is easily remedied.

 Click on the Zoom Out button on the toolbar until you have the whole project in view

	ⓘ	Task Name	Duration	Start	Jul '07	Aug '07	Sep '07	Oct '07	Nov '07
1		− Initiation Stage	12 days	Mon 7/2/07					
2		Agree Project Objectives	1 day	Mon 7/2/07					
3		Identify Stakeholders	1 day	Tue 7/3/07					
4		Select Project Team	2 days	Wed 7/4/07					
5		Identify Business Case	2 days	Fri 7/6/07					
6		Analyze the Risks	1 day	Fri 7/6/07					
7		Produce Outline Project Plan	1 day	Tue 7/10/07					
8		Project Approval	5 days	Wed 7/11/07	7/17				
9		− Strategy Stage	20 days	Wed 7/18/07					
10		Dummy Task	20 days	Wed 7/18/07					
11		− Analysis Stage	20 days	Wed 8/15/07					
12		Dummy Task	20 days	Wed 8/15/07					
13		− Design & Build Stage	20 days	Wed 9/12/07					
14		Dummy Task	20 days	Wed 9/12/07					
15		− Implementation Stage	20 days	Wed 10/10/07					
16		Dummy Task	20 days	Wed 10/10/07					

Select Show Outline Level 1 from the toolbar, to display the top-level view of your project, with just the stages showing

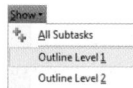

	ⓘ	Task Name	Duration	Start	Jul '07	Aug '07	Sep '07	Oct '07	Nov '07
1		+ Initiation Stage	12 days	Mon 7/2/07					
9		+ Strategy Stage	20 days	Wed 7/18/07					
11		+ Analysis Stage	20 days	Wed 8/15/07					
13		+ Design & Build Stage	20 days	Wed 9/12/07					
15		+ Implementation Stage	20 days	Wed 10/10/07					

Now select Show All Subtasks from the toolbar and use the Zoom In button from the toolbar to get back to the task details. You may also need to use the Windows scrollbars (shown at the bottom of the illustration below) to get the focus back to the required time period

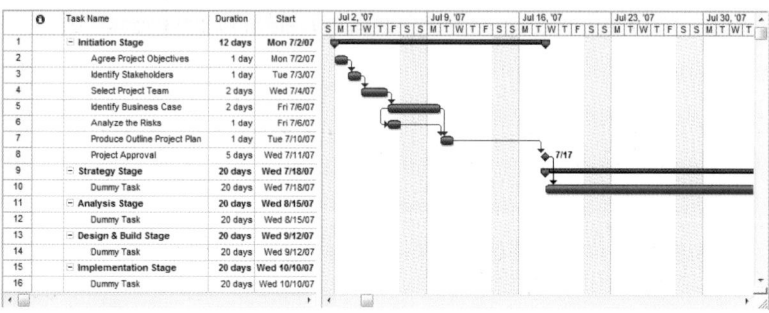

Contingency

When you first start a project you may be able to identify some of the key tasks. But there will still be a lot of unknown factors, particularly in the later project stages. To cope with this, and still be able to produce an outline schedule, you will need to put in some sort of allowance or contingency figure.

How Much?

How much contingency should you add to cope with these unknown factors? There is no sure answer, but the rule of thumb that seems to work for the author, for medium-sized projects (typically 6 to 9 months' duration), is:

- Add 100% to your initial estimate (yes, double it)

- When you get to the end of the Strategy stage and estimate the remaining work on the project, add 50%

- At the end of the Analysis stage add 25%

What you will be doing through the project is identifying more tasks. So spread your contingency figure across all the stages, with the highest amount where you have the least certainty. As you identify these additional tasks and add them to the plan, you can reduce your contingency. At the end of each stage your contingency figure for that stage will have done its job.

Adding Contingency

Before you put in your contingency figure it is a good idea to make sure you have identified any key tasks for each stage. Then you can put these in at the same time as the contingency.

1 Click on the dummy task in a stage and insert any key tasks you can identify, then change it to Contingency and reduce it to balance the new tasks. The example below is for the Strategy stage and shows the contingency figure reduced to 6 days so the stage is still 20 days in total

	❶	Task Name	Duration	Start	Jul 16, '07	Jul 23, '07	Jul 30, '07	Aug 6, '07	Aug 13, '07
					S M T W T F S	S M T W T F S	S M T W T F S	S M T W T F S	S M T W T F S
8		Project Approval	5 days	Wed 7/11/07	7/17				
9		− Strategy Stage	20 days	Wed 7/18/07					
10		Carry Out Interviews	4 days	Wed 7/18/07					
11		Produce Draft Requirements	2 days	Tue 7/24/07					
12		Feedback Sessions	1 day	Thu 7/26/07					
13		Finalize Requirements	2 days	Fri 7/27/07					
14		Review Risks	2 days	Tue 7/31/07					
15		Produce Forward Plan	1 day	Thu 8/2/07					
16		Report to Management	2 days	Fri 8/3/07					
17		Contingency	6 days	Tue 8/7/07					
18		− Analysis Stage	20 days	Wed 8/15/07					
19		Dummy Task	20 days	Wed 8/15/07					

Visual Change Highlights

Visual change highlights is a new feature introduced in Project 2007. Any time you make a change to your project file, the tasks you change and any other tasks that are dependant on those changed tasks will be highlighted.

1 Select View>Show/Hide Change Highlighting or click the Highlighting button on the toolbar to turn highlighting on or off

2 Now click in the Duration field of a linked task, change the duration and press Enter

	❶	Task Name	Duration	Start	Finish
1		− Initiation Stage	13 days	Mon 7/2/07	Wed 7/18/07
2		Agree Project Objectives	1 day	Mon 7/2/07	Mon 7/2/07
3		Identify Stakeholders	2 days	Tue 7/3/07	Wed 7/4/07
4		Select Project Team	2 days	Thu 7/5/07	Fri 7/6/07
5		Identify Business Case	2 days	Mon 7/9/07	Tue 7/10/07
6		Analyze the Risks	1 day	Mon 7/9/07	Mon 7/9/07
7		Produce Outline Project Plan	1 day	Wed 7/11/07	Wed 7/11/07
8		Project Approval	5 days	Thu 7/12/07	Wed 7/18/07
9		− Strategy Stage	20 days	Thu 7/19/07	Wed 8/15/07
10		Carry Out Interviews	4 days	Thu 7/19/07	Tue 7/24/07
11		Produce Draft Requirements	2 days	Wed 7/25/07	Thu 7/26/07
12		Feedback Sessions	1 day	Fri 7/27/07	Fri 7/27/07
13		Finalize Requirements	2 days	Mon 7/30/07	Tue 7/31/07
14		Review Risks	2 days	Wed 8/1/07	Thu 8/2/07
15		Produce Forward Plan	1 day	Fri 8/3/07	Fri 8/3/07
16		Report to Management	2 days	Mon 8/6/07	Tue 8/7/07
17		Contingency	6 days	Wed 8/8/07	Wed 8/15/07

3 The divider bar between the table (on the left) and the Gantt chart (on the right) is highlighted in black in the above illustration. Drag this across to the right to expose the Finish column in the table

Notice that the duration of the task you have changed is highlighted (with a blue background) as is the duration of the stage (summary task). The start date of all the tasks that are dependant on it are also highlighted, as they have changed.

The finish date of the stage is highlighted as it has changed, as have all the finish dates of the dependant tasks. This feature allows you to see the impact of any changes you make so that you can undo them if necessary.

If you make further changes, Project will then highlight these new changes in place of the previous changes. If you undo new changes, the previous changes will again be highlighted.

Breaking Tasks Down

Once you have inserted summary tasks (Stages) as the first-level of the project WBS (Work Breakdown Structure), their constituent tasks become the second-level of the WBS. If you then need to break these tasks down into further subtasks, they become the third-level of the project WBS.

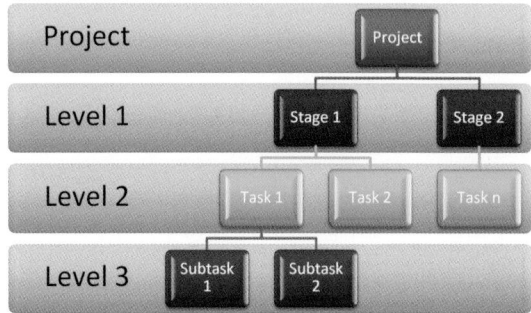

Task Size

The key question therefore becomes, how far should tasks be broken down into subtasks?

If you are to be able to estimate, schedule and control a task with any degree of accuracy, it needs to be small enough to enable you to do this. On the other hand a task needs to be large enough to be meaningful. One good definition of a task is that it should have a deliverable (it should produce something tangible) so that its completion can be confirmed.

There is one other useful rule of thumb. Although more than one person may work on a task, one person alone must be responsible for its completion. If not it will be a nightmare to control.

Based on those guidelines, conventional wisdom is that a task should be between 1 and 10 days' work effort (typically between 3 and 5 days) although its duration could be longer. If it is any larger then you should consider if it can be broken down into further subtasks. If it is smaller than 1 day, then see if it could be combined with another task.

However at the end of the day it is up to you, as the project manager, to make the decision. These are just guidelines, they are not rules. If you want a 20 day task and it makes sense in the context of your project, then that is fine, it's your decision.

Outline Numbering

For smaller projects with around a dozen tasks, the Task ID is probably a good enough way of keeping track of your tasks. But as your project starts to build up in size, you will want to be able to hide and show tasks and still keep track of where everything fits. Outline numbering gives you a simple way of achieving this.

1 Click on Tools>Options on the menu bar and the Options dialog box will open

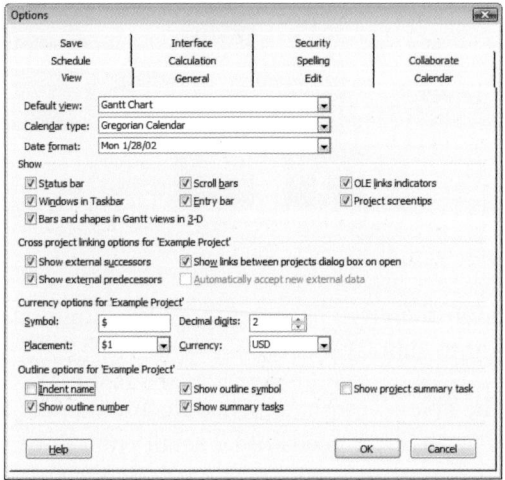

2 Make sure the View tab is selected, then (at the bottom left) check Show outline number and uncheck Indent name, then click OK

3 Show the subtasks for a stage

	ⓘ	Task Name	Duration	Start	Jul 2, '07							Jul 9, '07						
					S	S	M	T	W	T	F	S	S	M	T	W	T	F	S
1		⊟ 1 Initiation Stage	13 days	Mon 7/2/07														
2		1.1 Agree Project Objectives	1 day	Mon 7/2/07														
3		1.2 Identify Stakeholders	2 days	Tue 7/3/07														
4		1.3 Select Project Team	2 days	Thu 7/5/07														
5		1.4 Identify Business Case	2 days	Mon 7/9/07														
6		1.5 Analyze the Risks	1 day	Mon 7/9/07														
7		1.6 Produce Outline Project Plan	1 day	Wed 7/11/07														
8		1.7 Project Approval	5 days	Thu 7/12/07														

Your stages and tasks are now numbered in a structured format. Additional subtasks below task 1.4 will be numbered 1.4.1, 1.4.2 and so on.

Hot tip

Removing indenting also means you don't need to make the Task Name column so wide.

Subtasks

Creating subtasks is a similar process to creating summary tasks, but instead of inserting a summary task and outdenting it, you insert the subtasks and indent them.

1 Select the task in front of which you wish to insert the subtasks (i.e. after the task that they will be subtasks of) and press the Insert key once for each new subtask

	ⓘ	Task Name	Duration	Start	Jul 16, '07 S M T W T F S	Jul 23, '07 S M T W T F S
9		− 2 Strategy Stage	20 days	Wed 7/18/07		
10		2.1 Carry Out Interviews	4 days	Wed 7/18/07		
11						
12						
13		2.2 Produce Draft Requirements	2 days	Tue 7/24/07		
14		2.3 Feedback Sessions	1 day	Thu 7/26/07		

2 Then type in the new subtask names and their durations (in the example Interview Managers and Interview Staff)

	ⓘ	Task Name	Duration	Start	Jul 16, '07 S M T W T F S	Jul 23, '07 S M T W T F S	Jul 30, '07 S M T W T F S
9		− 2 Strategy Stage	24 days	Wed 7/18/07			
10		2.1 Carry Out Interviews	4 days	Wed 7/18/07			
11		2.2 Interview Managers	2 days	Tue 7/24/07			
12		2.3 Interview Staff	2 days	Thu 7/26/07			
13		2.4 Produce Draft Requirements	2 days	Mon 7/30/07			

Notice that they have been treated as tasks at the moment and have therefore extended the project by another four days.

3 Now select the two tasks by Ctrl+clicking on their Task Names or Task IDs and click the Indent button on the toolbar

	ⓘ	Task Name	Duration	Start	Jul 16, '07 S M T W T F S	Jul 23, '07 S M T W T F S	Jul 30, '07 S M T W T F S
9		− 2 Strategy Stage	20 days	Wed 7/18/07			
10		− 2.1 Carry Out Interviews	4 days	Wed 7/18/07			
11		2.1.1 Interview Managers	2 days	Wed 7/18/07			
12		2.1.2 Interview Staff	2 days	Fri 7/20/07			
13		2.2 Produce Draft Requirements	2 days	Tue 7/24/07			
14		2.3 Feedback Sessions	1 day	Thu 7/26/07			
15		2.4 Finalize Requirements	2 days	Fri 7/27/07			
16		2.5 Review Risks	2 days	Tue 7/31/07			
17		2.6 Produce Forward Plan	1 day	Thu 8/2/07			
18		2.7 Report to Management	2 days	Fri 8/3/07			
19		2.8 Contingency	6 days	Tue 8/7/07			

The two subtasks have now been numbered 2.1.1 and 2.1.2, their summary task 2.1 is now in bold and the schedule is restored.

Hot tip

Subtasks can be shown and hidden by clicking the + or - to the left of their summary task name or using the Show button on the toolbar.

Summary

- The way the tasks in a project are structured is referred to as a Work Breakdown Structure (WBS). The best approach is to break the project down one stage and one level at a time as more information becomes known

- A summary task is any task that has subtasks beneath it, and, with multiple levels, a task can be both a subtask and a summary task. Outdenting promotes a task to a summary task and Indenting demotes it to a subtask

- The first-level tasks in a structure are normally called the project Stages and are always summary tasks. There will normally be between three and eight stages in a project and a standard set of five is provided as a starting point

- Stages are created in a project by inserting them as tasks and then indenting the tasks beneath them to make them subtasks of the stage

- As you start to build up your project structure you can zoom in and out and show different outline levels to move between the big picture and the detail

- At the start of a project it is important to add contingency to reflect the unknown things that will only be discovered during the project. Contingency is best added by stage to reflect how much or little is known about that stage

- Visual change highlights can be turned on or off. When on, it provides an excellent way of seeing the impact of any changes that are made

- Tasks need to be small enough to estimate, schedule and control but large enough to be meaningful and produce a deliverable. In general terms they should be between 1 day and 10 days work effort

- Outline numbering can give a better reference (which reflects the WBS) to tasks than the task ID

- Subtasks are created by inserting new tasks below an existing task and then indenting them

6 More About Tasks

This chapter goes into Tasks in a little more detail. It introduces lag time and lead time, task notes, setting deadline dates, critical path and moving linked tasks.

Lag Time and Lead Time

Up to now we have been linking tasks, mainly in a finish-to-start dependency, with the next task starting immediately after the preceding task finishes. However, there are times when you will want the tasks to have a gap or overlap between them and we do this using lag time and lead time.

Lag Time

Lag time is when there is a gap (or lag) between the finish of one task and the start of the next task. This is input using the Lag time field on the Task Dependency dialog box. In the following example we want to introduce a 2 day lag between the end of Task 1.1 Agree Project Objectives and the start of Task 1.2 Identify Stakeholders.

	❶	Task Name	Duration	Start	Jul 2, '07 S M T W T F S
1		⊟ **1 Initiation Stage**	**12 days**	**Mon 7/2/07**	
2		1.1 Agree Project Objectives	1 day	Mon 7/2/07	
3		1.2 Identify Stakeholders	1 day	Tue 7/3/07	
4		1.3 Select Project Team	2 days	Wed 7/4/07	

1 Double-click on the line connecting the two tasks where you want to add lag time to open the Task Dependency dialog box

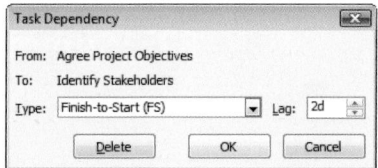

2 Change the Lag time using the spinner controls or by typing in the required duration and click OK

1		⊟ **1 Initiation Stage**	**14 days**	**Mon 7/2/07**	
2		1.1 Agree Project Objectives	1 day	Mon 7/2/07	
3		1.2 Identify Stakeholders	1 day	Thu 7/5/07	
4		1.3 Select Project Team	2 days	Fri 7/6/07	

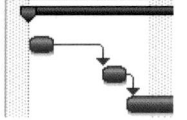

The dependent task will be rescheduled and the link line will be extended to the length of the lag time. Any other tasks linked to the dependant task will also be rescheduled by Project.

Lead Time

Lead time is where there is an overlap, with the next task starting before the previous task has finished. This is also input using the Lag time field, but using a negative number to represent lead time. In the following example we want to introduce a 1 day lead time between Task 1.3 Select Project Team and Task 1.4 Identify Business Case.

	ⓘ	Task Name	Duration	Start	Jul 2, '07	Jul 9, '07
1		▬ 1 Initiation Stage	14 days	Mon 7/2/07		
2		1.1 Agree Project Objectives	1 day	Mon 7/2/07		
3		1.2 Identify Stakeholders	1 day	Thu 7/5/07		
4		1.3 Select Project Team	2 days	Fri 7/6/07		
5		1.4 Identify Business Case	2 days	Tue 7/10/07		
6		1.5 Analyze the Risks	1 day	Tue 7/10/07		
7		1.6 Produce Outline Project Plan	1 day	Thu 7/12/07		
8		1.7 Project Approval	5 days	Fri 7/13/07		

1 Double-click on the connecting line between the two tasks where you want to include lead time to open the Task Dependency dialog box

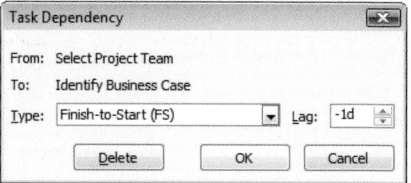

2 Change the Lag time using the down spinner control or type a negative number to represent the lead time duration and click OK

	ⓘ	Task Name	Duration	Start	Jul 2, '07	Jul 9, '07
4		1.3 Select Project Team	2 days	Fri 7/6/07		
5		1.4 Identify Business Case	2 days	Mon 7/9/07		
6		1.5 Analyze the Risks	1 day	Mon 7/9/07		
7		1.6 Produce Outline Project Plan	1 day	Wed 7/11/07		
8		1.7 Project Approval	5 days	Thu 7/12/07		

The dependent task has been brought forward and now starts one day before the preceding task finishes. In the above example the task following the dependant task has also been brought forward to overlap by one day due to its start-to-start dependency.

Task Drivers

Task drivers allow you to view the constraints and dependencies that impact a task's start date. They can help you to establish the factor or factors that may be delaying a task, such as task dependency, calendar constraints, schedule date, holidays or vacation.

 In Gantt chart view click on the Task Drivers button in the toolbar to open the task drivers panel to the left of the task sheet

In the example above, the task driver panel displays the name and start date of the selected task. It also contains details of the predecessor task(s), the dependency type, any lag time and the project or resource calendar(s) that are applied. The predecessor task(s) and calendar(s) are active hypertext links (shown in blue).

 Click on the predecessor task name to back-track to that task

 Click on the calendar name to display the relevant resource or project calendar

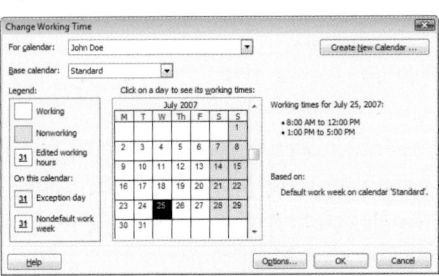

Hot tip

Calendars are covered in chapter 9.

Task Notes

Task notes can be attached to any task to record additional, free text information. You can add a task note to a task in Gantt chart view or any other view where the task note button is active.

1 Select the task that you wish to add the task note to by clicking on the task name

2 Click the Task Note button on the toolbar to open the Task Information dialog box (at the Notes tab)

3 Type in your note and format it if required (using the format buttons above the typing area), then click OK to add the note to the task

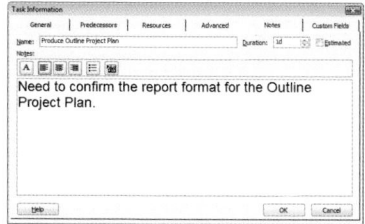

4 Now pause your mouse pointer over the yellow note symbol in the Information box to display the note

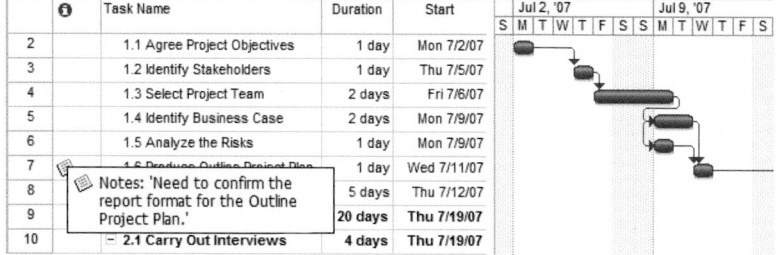

5 To edit the note or add further text to it just double-click the yellow note symbol in the information box. This will reopen the task information box at the note

6 To delete a note just delete all the note text in the task information dialog box

You can also access task notes text by double-clicking on the task name (or clicking the Task Information button on the toolbar) and selecting the Notes tab.

Deadline Dates

Deadline dates can be set on a task to indicate a date by which the task must be completed. If at any time the task slips, so that it will not be completed by its deadline date, a warning indicator will be displayed in the information box for the task.

Deadline dates are for information only and do not have any impact on the scheduling process. They should not be confused with task constraints (dealt with in chapter 11) which can determine when a task will be scheduled. Deadline dates are set on the Advanced tab of the Task Information dialog box.

1 In Gantt chart view, double-click on the task you want to set a deadline for and the Task Information dialog box will open

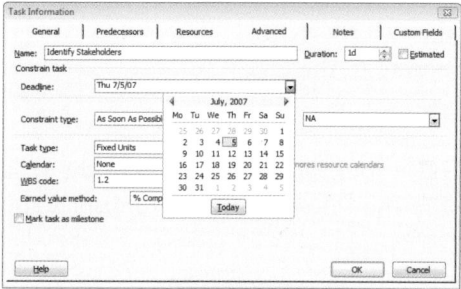

2 Select the Advanced tab, click on the down arrow beside Deadline, select your deadline date and click OK. The deadline is indicated on the Gantt chart by a green and white arrow symbol (see below)

	ⓘ	Task Name	Duration	Start	Jul 2, '07
					S M T W T F S
1		1 Initiation Stage	11 days	Mon 7/2/07	
2		1.1 Agree Project Objectives	1 day	Mon 7/2/07	
3		1.2 Identify Stakeholders	1 day	Tue 7/3/07	

3 If the task slips past its deadline date, a warning indicator will be displayed. Position your cursor over the warning indicator to display the details

3	❶	1.2 Identify Stakeholders	1 day	Fri 7/6/07	
4		❶ This task finishes on Fri 7/6/07 which is later than its Deadline on Thu 7/5/07	2 days	Mon 7/9/07	
5			2 days	Tue 7/10/07	
6		1.5 Analyze the Risks	1 day	Tue 7/10/07	

Moving Around

As your project starts to build up, you will soon reach a point when you will not be able to see all the project information in one view, particularly in Gantt chart view. As well as zooming in and out (which was covered in chapter 5), you will also need to be able to move around the view.

Scrollbars

You can use the scrollbars and sliders to move around vertically and horizontally. Gantt chart view has one vertical scrollbar (on the right-hand side of the screen), which moves the task sheet and the Gantt chart information up and down. It has two horizontal scrollbars (at the bottom of the screen) which move the task sheet and the chart left and right independently of each other.

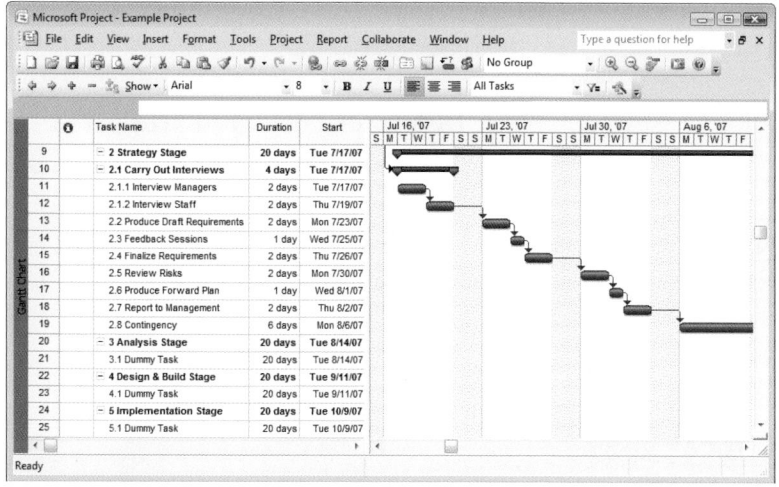

Scroll To Task

When moving around with the scrollbars, it is quite easy to loose all sight of the Gantt chart part of the view. A useful short-cut is the Scroll To Task button which will bring the appropriate part of the Gantt chart into view.

 Click on the task you want to bring into view in the task sheet and click the Scroll To Task button on the toolbar

The Gantt chart will scroll to bring the bar for the selected task into view on the right-hand side of the screen.

Hot tip

You can use Ctrl+Home to get back to the top left-hand corner of any view.

Critical Path

The Critical Path is the term given to the sequence of tasks that are critical to the duration of the project. A Critical Task is one that, if delayed or lengthened, will directly affect the project finish date.

The following diagram represents a simple project consisting of four tasks. Tasks A, B and D are each of two days' duration, while Task C is of one day's duration. Tasks B and C are both dependent on Task A with finish-to-start relationships. Task D is dependent on both Tasks B and C, again with finish-to-start relationships. Assuming no lag time, the total duration of the project is six days.

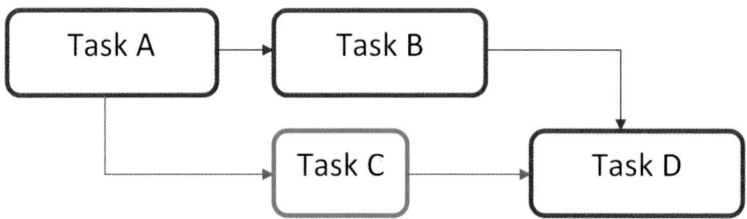

Non-critical Tasks
Even if Task C were to slip by one day it would still not impact the completion of Task D and therefore the project would still be completed in six days. Task C is therefore deemed to be a non-critical task.

Critical Tasks
On the other hand, if any of Tasks A, B or D were to slip by one day the project would take seven days to complete and these tasks are therefore deemed to be critical tasks.

Critical Path
The Critical Path is the path through the project that links all of the Critical Tasks. In the diagram above, the Critical Path (shown by the red line and red boxes) consists of Task A, the link between Task A and Task B, Task B, the link between Task B and Task D, and finally Task D.

Calculating the Critical Path
In Project the Critical Path is calculated using the Gantt Chart Wizard. This is covered in the next topic.

Gantt Chart Wizard

The critical path through the project is calculated using the Gantt Chart Wizard. The default when setting the critical path is that the critical path and tasks will be displayed in red and non-critical tasks and path in blue.

1 With your project in Gantt chart view, click the Gantt Chart Wizard button on the toolbar and the Gantt Chart Wizard will open

2 Click Next to move past the welcome message

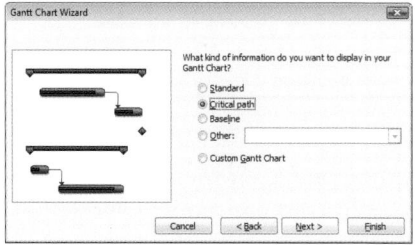

3 Select the critical path (second radio button down) as in the above example and click Next

4 Click Next twice more unless you want to change any of the defaults

5 Click Format It and then Exit Wizard and your Gantt chart is now formatted to show the critical path

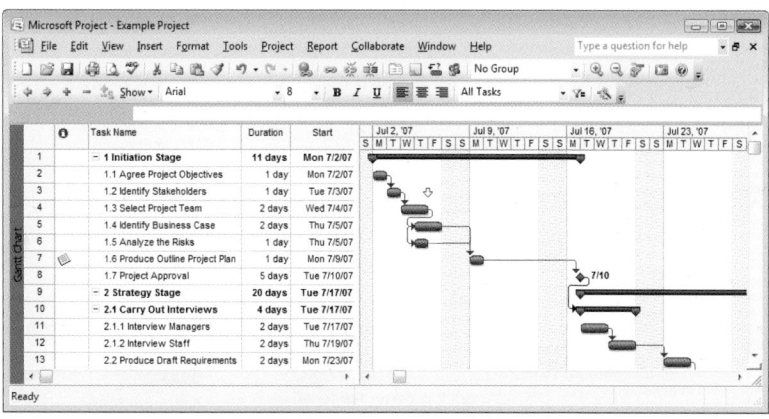

Splitting Tasks

Normally a task will be worked on from start to finish. But you can split a task if it needs to be interrupted and finished at a later time. In the following example, Task 2.1.1 Interview Managers needs to be split as half of the managers are going to be on a conference the week it has been scheduled.

1 With your project in Gantt chart view, click on the Split Task button on the toolbar and a pop-up asks you to select the split point

11		2.1.1 Interview Managers	2 days	Tue 7/17/07	
12					
13		Split Task:			
14		Start:		Wed 7/18/07	
15		Click the mouse to insert a split on the task.			

2 Position the pointer on the task bar where you want to make the split (the pop-up will show the date where the split will start, as in the example above) and click. The task will be split with a 1 day gap

11		2.1.1 Interview Managers	2 days	Tue 7/17/07	
12		2.1.2 Interview Staff	2 days	Fri 7/20/07	
13		2.2 Produce Draft Requirements	2 days	Tue 7/24/07	

3 You can now drag the right-hand part of the task bar, on the Gantt chart, to the right, to increase the gap

	ⓘ	Task Name	Duration	Start	Jul 16, '07 S M T W T F S	Jul 23, '07 S M T W T F S
9		− **2 Strategy Stage**	23 days	Tue 7/17/07		
10		− **2.1 Carry Out Interviews**	7 days	Tue 7/17/07		
11		2.1.1 Interview Managers	2 days	Tue 7/17/07		
12		2.1.2 Interview Staff	2 days	Tue 7/24/07		
13		2.2 Produce Draft Requirements	2 days	Thu 7/26/07		
14		2.3 Feedback Sessions	1 day	Mon 7/30/07		

4 To remove a split, just drag the right-hand piece of the task bar back so that it joins the left-hand piece again

	ⓘ	Task Name	Duration	Start	Jul 16, '07 S M T W T F S	Jul 23, '07 S M T W T F S
11		2.1.1 Interview Managers	2 days	Tue 7/17/07		
12		2.1.2 Interview Staff	2 days	Thu 7/19/07		
13		2.2 Produce Draft Requirements	2 days	Mon 7/23/07		

Moving Linked Tasks

In the previous topic we dragged part of a split task to move it backwards or forward in time. We can do the same thing with any task but if the task is linked it may cause a scheduling conflict. In the following example we will move the task after the split task back to use the available time.

	ⓘ	Task Name	Duration	Start	Jul 16, '07								Jul 23, '07					
					S	M	T	W	T	F	S	S	M	T	W	T	F	S
10		⊟ 2.1 Carry Out Interviews	7 days	Tue 7/17/07														
11		2.1.1 Interview Managers	2 days	Tue 7/17/07														
12		2.1.2 Interview Staff	2 days	Tue 7/24/07														
13		2.2 Produce Draft Requirements	2 days	Thu 7/26/07														

1 Position your cursor over the task bar of the task you want to move (the cursor will turn into a 4-headed arrow) then drag the task bar back to where you want it to start and release the mouse key

2 If a planning wizard appears (as illustrated right), select Remove the link and click OK. The task will be unlinked and moved to where you dragged it (Cancel will undo the move)

3 Relink the tasks as appropriate. In the example below the moved task 2.1.2 stayed linked to the following task 2.2, so the preceding task 2.1.1 (which had lost its link in step 2) has also been linked to the following task 2.2

	ⓘ	Task Name	Duration	Start	Jul 16, '07								Jul 23, '07					
					S	M	T	W	T	F	S	S	M	T	W	T	F	S
10		⊟ 2.1 Carry Out Interviews	5 days	Tue 7/17/07														
11		2.1.1 Interview Managers	2 days	Tue 7/17/07														
12	🔲	2.1.2 Interview Staff	2 days	Wed 7/18/07														
13		2.2 Produce Draft Requirements	2 days	Tue 7/24/07														
14		2.3 Feedback Sessions	1 day	Thu 7/26/07														

Note in the example above that the moved task is now no longer on the critical path, so it has turned blue. There is also a calendar symbol in the task information box (indicating a constraint). If you position your cursor over it, the constraint will be displayed.

Summary

- Lag Time and Lead Time are used to create gaps (lag time) and overlaps (lead time) between tasks. The lag or lead time is indicated by the length of the line linking the two tasks on the Gantt chart

- Task Drivers allow you to view the constraints, dependencies and calendars that impact a task's start date and you can follow these links to investigate any issues

- Task notes can be attached to any task and are indicated by a note symbol in the task's information box. They can be read, amended and deleted by double-clicking the note symbol or by double-clicking the task name and selecting the Note tab

- Deadline dates can be attached to any task that has a deadline. While they do not affect the scheduling, they will trigger a warning in the task information box if the task slips and is going to miss the deadline

- Moving around the Gantt chart can be done using the scrollbars but the Scroll To Task button provides a useful shortcut for getting a task's task bar into view

- Another useful shortcut is Ctrl+Home which will move to the top left-hand corner of the task sheet

- A critical task is one that will, if delayed, delay the final completion of the project. The Critical Path is the path through the project that links all the critical tasks

- Gantt Chart Wizard is the process, in Project, that is used for setting (or removing) the critical path (it can also be used for changing some of the defaults)

- Splitting a task allows the task to be split into two (or more) sections with gaps of any required duration between them

- Tasks can be moved by dragging their task bar on the Gantt chart, however, if the task is linked, this may lead to a scheduling conflict. The best way to deal with this is to remove the link causing the conflict, move the task and then relink it as required

7 Resources

Up to now we have dealt with planning a project and defining the tasks needed to carry it out. This chapter introduces the organization of a project and working with project resources.

Organizing a Project

Organization is a key area for a project manager. If you are not organized you will quickly loose track of what's happening on your project.

Having established what your project has to produce (the deliverables) you should have planned the project by producing a work breakdown structure and started to identify the work (tasks) that will need to be carried out to produce the deliverables. The next step is to organize the resources you will need to complete the tasks.

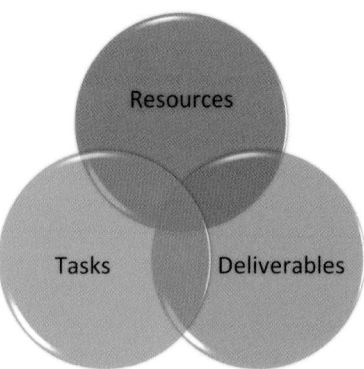

Resources

Resources represent the people, material and facilities that you will use on your project. As you will have seen in previous chapters, it is quite possible to plan and schedule a project without assigning resources to it. In fact, if you are going to be doing all the work on a project yourself, you may not bother to allocate resources (yourself) to the project. On the other hand, if you have other, non-project, work to deal with, or you will be using other people and things on your project, then it will be much easier to organize if you allocate resources.

Resource Information

You can store lots of information about the resources you will use in Project. Anything from peoples' availability (resource calendar) to costs and even their email addresses.

Fortunately, setting up the resources and the associated resource information and then allocating the resources to tasks is a very straightforward operation in Project.

Project Stakeholders

The major resources on most projects will be people: the people who will be involved in the project and the people who will do the work. But there are also other people with a vested interest in the outcome of a project: people who will be impacted by it in some way. They could include your management, staff affected by any changes and even your suppliers and customers. The generic term for all these people and groups is "project stakeholders".

Stakeholder List

It is a good idea to start out by making a list of all your project stakeholders. You may not need to enter them all as resources but you should certainly keep the list available as you will probably need to think about communicating with them about the project every so often.

So produce a list of your project stakeholders. Ensure you include:

- Your project sponsor, steering group or whoever you report to about the project

- Your project team (the people who will be working with you on completing the tasks)

- Any other people in the business who will be affected by the outcome of the project

- Customers and suppliers (both internal and external) who will be affected by the outcome of the project

- Anyone else who could be affected by the project or who could have an impact on it

Communication Plan

When you have identified them all, think about the impact that they could have on your project. If they could have an impact in any way then you need to make sure you communicate what's happening on the project to them. That's called producing a communication plan.

The FUD Factor

Finally, remember that no-one likes being kept in the dark and that's where the dreaded FUD (Fear, Uncertainty and Doubt) Factor creeps in. After all, you want them all on your side, not against you when the chips are down!

Allocating Resources

People who are assigned to a project are usually assigned on some form of temporary basis. That is, they will be working on your project for a set period of time. They will usually have other jobs and they may even have to keep on doing those other jobs, for part of the time, while they are also working on your project.

If you have a person allocated to your project on anything less than a full-time basis, you will need to take account of their other work commitments. This will sometimes be on the basis of their being allocated to the project for a certain number of days per week or month. Or it might be on the basis of their being allocated to the project for a percentage of their time (typically, 50% to 80%).

It will be very important to get a firm agreement on any part-time allocations up front, as you may need to fight for key resources at critical times. These are the sort of factors that need to be recorded as part of your project planning document.

The question is: how many days will a person work per week or per month on your project? If you know exactly when they will be available day by day then you can work that way. If not, you need some sort of rule to work to. Something that allows for them to be on vacation, on training courses, off sick, attending company meetings, etc. As a rule of thumb you could use the following:

THERE ARE 52 WEEKS IN A YEAR, BUT…	
- 3 weeks for annual vacation	49 weeks
- 2 weeks for public holidays	47 weeks
- 2 weeks for illness	45 weeks
- 2 weeks for training	43 weeks
- 1 week for other work-related things	42 weeks
- 2 weeks for wasted time	40 weeks
Leaves just 200 days for work, at best!	

So if people are allocated to your project full-time you will get less than 4 days' work a week from them. If they are not allocated full-time you will get proportionally less. Allocate people and schedule them on this basis (rather than 5 days a week) and you will not get caught out in the resource trap.

Resource Sheet

The Resource Sheet is where you enter details of the people and other resources you will be using on your project. It is called a sheet as it functions in a similar way to a spreadsheet. It can be accessed by clicking on Resource Sheet on the View Bar or by selecting View>Resource Sheet from the Menu.

1 To enter a person, click in the first Resource Name field and enter the name of your first resource (it's a good idea to start with yourself)

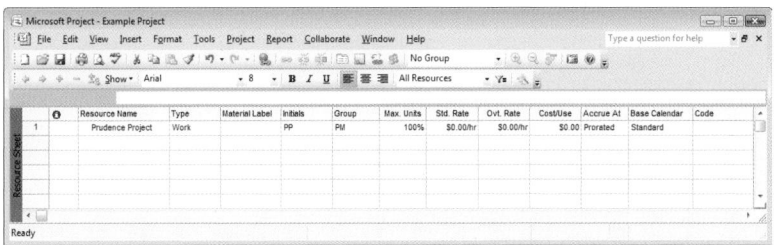

The Type defaults to Work, the Max Units to 100% (the full resource is available to the project) and the Base Calendar to Standard. Costs are dealt with in the next chapter and, initially, it is best to leave these defaults as they are.

2 Add the Initials, and Group if required and then add in the other people resources, as in the following example

	ⓘ	Resource Name	Type	Material Label	Initials	Group
1		Prudence Project	Work		PP	Proj Mgr
2		Joe Soap	Work		JS	Marketing
3		Mary Dee	Work		MD	Finance
4		Wendy Page	Work		WP	IT
5		Bill Buggs	Work		BB	Executive

Once you have created the initial resource sheet information, you can go back any time and change the details in any field. You can add new resources to the end of the resource sheet or insert new resources in the middle (just click on the resource name you wish to insert the new resource in front of and press the Insert key).

You can also delete a resource by clicking on the Resource ID (the number on the left-hand side of the sheet) and pressing Delete.

Hot tip

The Group field does not have to be used for group or department, you can use it for anything you want to be able to extract information on.

Resource Information

In addition to inputting information into the Resource Sheet, you can add additional resource information through the Resource Information dialog box.

1 On the Resource Sheet view, select the name of the resource you wish to add additional information on and click the Resource Information button on the Toolbar to open the Resource Information dialog box, as below

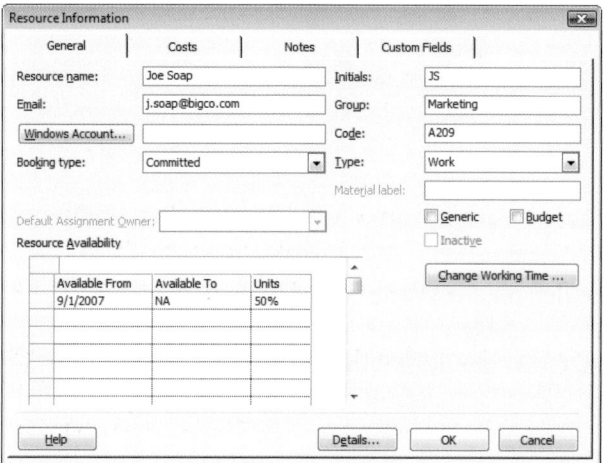

2 On the General tab, you can change any of the information you input to the Resource Sheet and also add information on their email address, and availability

3 For example, in the example above, Joe is not going to be available to the project until September and then he will only be available for 50% of the time

The other fields on the General tab are Windows Account (to look up someone on your network); Booking Type (Committed or Proposed if someone is only provisionally allocated); Generic (for a resource type where there may be a team of people providing the work); Budget (for financial resources); Change Working Time (access to their calendar); and Details (to look up their details from your Outlook address book). Where relevant, these fields are dealt with in later topics.

Material & Cost Resources

In addition to work resources (people), you can also put in material resources (for consumable materials or supplies) and cost resources (where the cost is not dependant on the work or duration of a task).

1. Open your project file in Resource Sheet view and add in any material resources you will be using

	ⓘ	Resource Name	Type	Material Label	Initials	Group	Max. Units
1		Prudence Project	Work		PP	Proj Mgr	100%
2		Joe Soap	Work		JS	Marketing	0%
3		Mary Dee	Work		MD	Finance	100%
4		Wendy Page	Work		WP	IT	100%
5		Bill Buggs	Work		BB	Executive	100%
6		Paint	Material	gallon		Facilities	
7		Carpet	Material	square yard		Facilities	

Note in the above illustration that Joe Soap has 0% Max Units. This is the result of changing his availability in the previous topic. It will show 0% until September, then it will show 50%.

2. Now select a material resource and click on the Resource Information button on the Toolbar. Notice on the General tab that all the work-related fields are deselected

3. Select the Costs tab and note there are two cost fields: Standard Rate (used where the cost is dependant on the quantity used) and Per Use Cost (a one-off cost for using the resource)

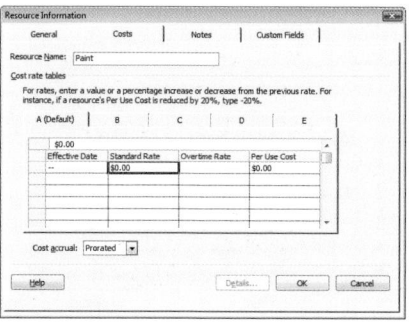

Cost Resources

Cost resources are the third type of resource and they are used for costs that are unrelated to the work effort or duration of a task. This would typically be for costs like travel and expenses that could be applied to a number of different tasks. Cost resources are dealt with in the following chapter.

Resource Notes

Resource Notes can be attached to resources in a similar manner to attaching task notes to tasks.

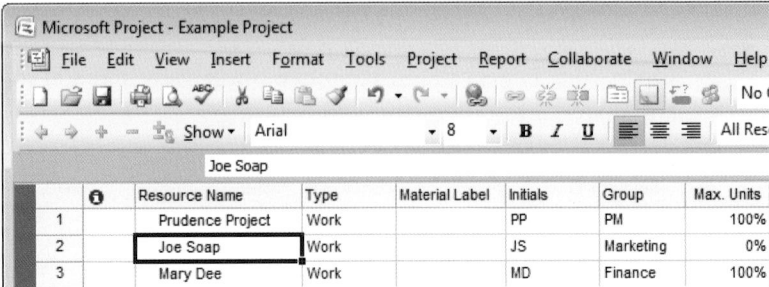

1 Select the Resource Name of the resource you want to attach the note to, click the yellow Note button on the Toolbar and the Resource Information dialog box opens at the Note tab

2 Type in your note, format it if required and click OK. The resource sheet now shows a note symbol in the Resource Information Box as illustrated below

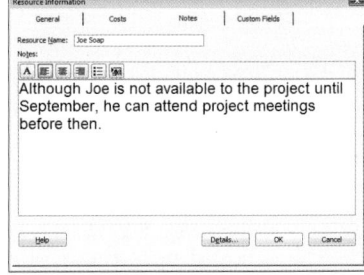

	ⓘ	Resource Name	Type	Material Label	Initials	Group	Max. Units
1		Prudence Project	Work		PP	Proj Mgr	100%
2	📝	Joe Soap	Work		JS	Marketing	0%
3		Mary Dee	Work		MD	Finance	100%
4					WP	IT	100%
5					BB	Executive	100%
6		Paint	Material	gallon		Facilities	

Notes: 'Although Joe is not available to the project until September, he can attend project meetings before then.'

3 Position your cursor over the note symbol to display the note, as illustrated above

The note can be edited by double-clicking on it and making any required changes. It can be deleted by double-clicking on it and deleting all the text. It can also be accessed by opening the Resource Information dialog box and selecting the Note tab.

Assigning Resources

Assigning resources is the process of allocating resources to tasks so that they can carry them out.

1 Open your project in Gantt chart view, select the task you wish to assign a resource to and click the Assign Resources button on the toolbar

2 When the Assign Resources dialog box opens, select the Resource Name of the resource you wish to assign to the task and click the Assign button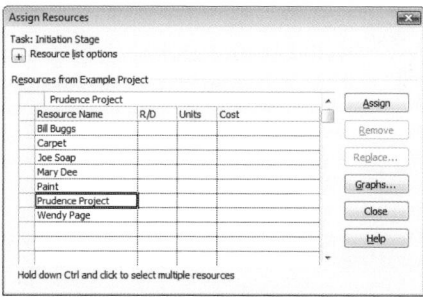

3 You can check a resource availability by selecting their name and clicking on the Graphs button, which will display their work loading as a graph

Beware

The Graphs feature is not available in versions before Project 2002.

Once resources have been assigned to tasks, the Gantt chart will display the names of the resources allocated to each task, as in the following illustration. Where resources have been allocated at 100% (the default) no percentage is shown on the Gantt chart. But if any resource is allocated at any other percentage, it is displayed after their name (as in task 1.3 below).

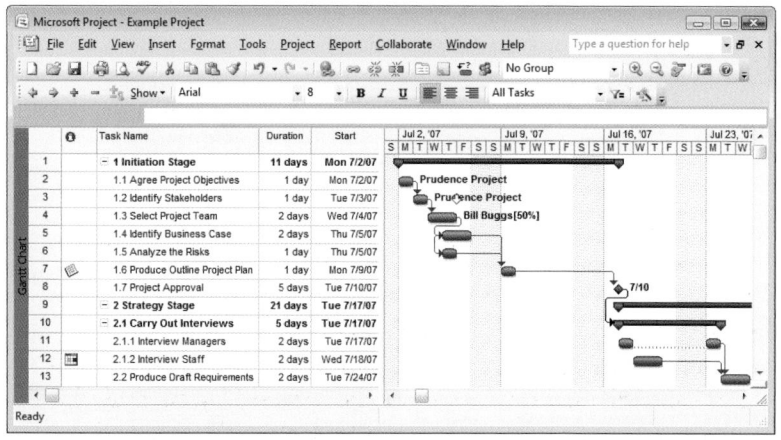

Multiple Resources

In many cases you will just be assigning a single resource to each task (which is the best way of controlling a project). However, sometimes you may need to assign two or more resources to tasks.

1 Select the task you want to assign multiple resources to and click the Assign Resources button on the toolbar

2 Select the first Resource Name in the Assign Resources dialog box and click the Assign button (the resource will be assigned as in the previous topic)

3 Now select and assign the second resource

92

	❶	Task Name	Duration	Start	Jul 2, '07 S M T W T F S	Jul 9, '07 S M T W T F S
1		− **1 Initiation Stage**	**10 days**	**Mon 7/2/07**		
2		1.1 Agree Project Objectives	1 day	Mon 7/2/07	Prudence Project	
3		1.2 Identify Stakeholders	1 day	Tue 7/3/07	Prudence Project	
4	◈	1.3 Select Project Team	1 day	Wed 7/4/07	Bill Buggs,Prudence Project	
5		1.4 Identify Business Case	2 days	Wed 7/4/07		

Notice that both resources are now allocated to the task but that the duration will have reduced. This is due to the way that Project calculates the duration of a task. When we added the second resource the duration was halved (assuming both resources were allocated at 100%) and a warning symbol has been placed in the task information box.

4 Click on the warning symbol and select the second option to keep the original duration or the third option to reduce the hours each will work

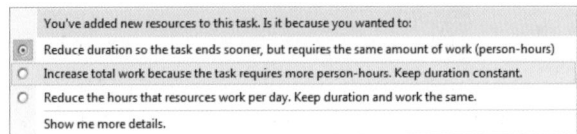
You've added new resources to this task. Is it because you wanted to:
- ● Reduce duration so the task ends sooner, but requires the same amount of work (person-hours)
- ○ Increase total work because the task requires more person-hours. Keep duration constant.
- ○ Reduce the hours that resources work per day. Keep duration and work the same.

Show me more details.

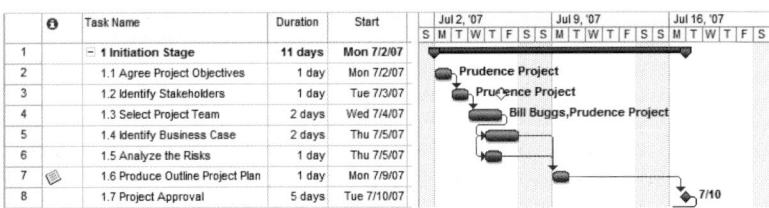

	❶	Task Name	Duration	Start	Jul 2, '07 S M T W T F S	Jul 9, '07 S M T W T F S	Jul 16, '07 S M T W T F S
1		− **1 Initiation Stage**	**11 days**	**Mon 7/2/07**			
2		1.1 Agree Project Objectives	1 day	Mon 7/2/07	Prudence Project		
3		1.2 Identify Stakeholders	1 day	Tue 7/3/07	Prudence Project		
4		1.3 Select Project Team	2 days	Wed 7/4/07	Bill Buggs,Prudence Project		
5		1.4 Identify Business Case	2 days	Thu 7/5/07			
6		1.5 Analyze the Risks	1 day	Thu 7/5/07			
7	🗎	1.6 Produce Outline Project Plan	1 day	Mon 7/9/07			
8		1.7 Project Approval	5 days	Tue 7/10/07			◆ 7/10

Multiple Tasks

In addition to being able to assign single and multiple resources to a task, you can also assign a resource to multiple tasks.

1 Select the tasks you wish to assign the resource to by holding down the Ctrl key and clicking on each task in turn (or by dragging across the task names if they are adjacent)

2 Now click on the Assign Resources button on the toolbar and assign the appropriate resource

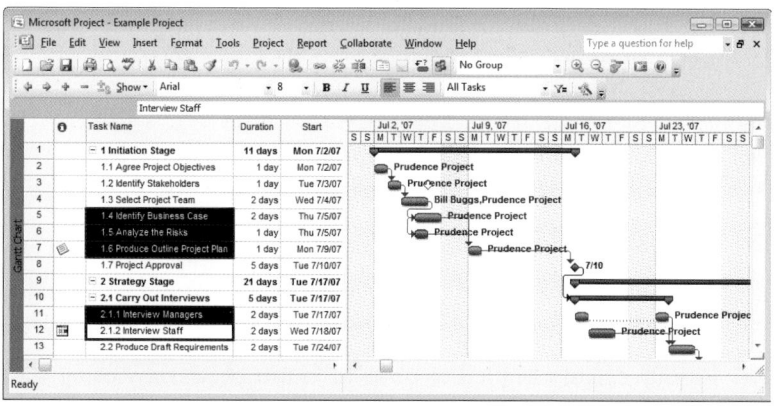

The resource has been allocated to all the selected tasks as in the above illustration. However, in the illustration above we have also created an overload situation. Tasks 1.3, 1.4, and 1.5 are all taking place on the same day which has created 24 hours of work for our project manager! This can be observed using the Graph button on the Resource Allocation dialog box.

3 To resolve this overload select Tools>Level Resources from the menu bar and click the Level Now button. The project will be rescheduled to correct the overload

Hot tip

Resource leveling is dealt with fully in chapter 11.

Summary

- Organizing a project involves allocating the people and other resources to the tasks in order to carry out the work and produce the project deliverables

- It is not essential to allocate resources to tasks and for a small project it may not be necessary or worthwhile

- Project stakeholders are the people who will be impacted by or have a vested interest in the outcome of your project. They all need to be identified so that you can plan what you will need to communicate to them during the project

- When it comes to allocating resources, remember that, on average, a person will deliver between 180 and 200 days effective work effort per year, if they are allocated to your project full-time

- Resource sheet view is the best place to input the basic details of your people and other project resources

- The resource information dialog box allows you to edit and add further resource information, including availability and working time

- Material resources can be used to allocate facilities and materials to the project together with their costs

- Resource notes can be added to any resource and show up as a note symbol in the resource information box. Notes can be edited or deleted by double-clicking the note symbol

- Resources are assigned to tasks in Gantt sheet view using the assign resources button on the toolbar

- Multiple resources can be assigned to a task and by default will reduce the duration of the task unless you tell Project to increase the work effort or reduce the hours worked on the task

- You can also allocate a resource to a number of tasks by selecting all the tasks and then selecting and assigning the relevant resource

8 Project Costs

This chapter looks at adding cost information to resources and tasks in order to build up the project budget. This can then be used to confirm the business case. It also introduces the management of risks.

Project Costs

One of the first questions a project manager gets asked is "How much is all this going to cost?" and it's usually only moments after being "given" the project in the first place!

No-one can be expected to produce a reliable cost estimate until they have a full grasp of the business requirements. This will only be available a couple of stages into the project. So, anything produced before then should be clearly identified as a preliminary estimate and issued with a corresponding "health warning".

Use Your Experts

The people in a business who are best able to produce accurate cost estimates will normally be in a Finance or Accounts section. Using them should not only save the project manager a lot of time, but should also ensure the accuracy of the figures. Some larger organizations will allocate a finance person to each project as a project accountant. But if you don't have that luxury you will have to do it as best you can yourself.

Costing

This is a guide to developing project costs without a project accountant. Take the internal people work effort (including any contingency) and cost it up (Project will do this for you). Add any other internal or external resource or material costs (again Project will help with this). Then add any recurring costs (the ongoing costs of operating the new whatever-it-is your project is delivering). We will look at each of these in turn:

Internal People Costs

If the business operates on a cost center principle, or charges clients for people's time, it may already have internal charging rates for its people. If not, they can be calculated.

Take the average annual salary for each grade of person working on the project (that way we don't have to know our colleagues' actual salaries!). Double it (to allow for premises and all the other costs of running the business) and divide it by 190 (as explained in the Allocating Resources topic) to get a daily internal cost. It is probably a good idea to check this figure with your finance people to see if they can come up with anything better.

This cost can be used to cost up the time each team member will spend on the project, to give the total internal people cost.

External People Costs

External people working on a project will usually be charging for their time in some way. It may be a fixed cost for providing a service or it may be on a daily or hourly rate. Whatever form it takes (and it should be specified in their contract or agreement), it can be used directly as the external people cost.

Other Project Costs

Every project will be different and consequently will be likely to involve different costs. However, these will typically include costs for a project office, furniture, computers, telephones, secretarial services, etc. There may be software costs (such as Project 2007), there may be a need to include travel and expenses (which can often be significant on a large or multi-location project) or any other appropriate costs.

Capital Costs

The costs of computers or other equipment, software packages or development, operating systems or database costs will normally be treated as capital (although the business may lease them). The relevant suppliers (or potential suppliers) should provide all of these costs for you. Your business will probably have a standard way of treating capital, depending on whether it leases or purchases and how it depreciates. Whichever way these are treated, they still need to be identified as project costs.

Revenue Operating Costs

Finally, there are the ongoing or operating costs of the new system, process or product which need to be determined for its expected lifetime. The annual depreciation charge for the capital costs should be determined by the business (see Capital Costs above). The other operating costs will need to be calculated. These could include staff (additional people to operate the new product or procedure), annual maintenance or support costs for hardware (computer or otherwise), annual support or maintenance for software, operating systems, database licenses and any other recurring costs in the project. It is important to recognize all these ongoing costs as they will need to be set against the expected business benefits in appraising the business case (or the justification for the project). This is not meant to be a complete list, just examples of the typical costs that may be applicable to your project.

Costs in Project

Having looked at some general considerations about costing in the previous topic, we will now look at how Project can help with these. Essentially Project should be able to handle all the (one-off) project-related costs but not the ongoing operating or revenue costs of any implemented solution.

Project treats costs under two headings: Resource Costs (costs related to the people and material resources you will use on the project) and Fixed Costs (not related to resource usage).

Resource Costs

Once you have identified all the stages, tasks and subtasks for a project, you will have estimated the work effort required to carry out the project. This should include the appropriate element of contingency (to deal with the unknown) based on where you are in the project. By adding resource costs for all the internal people who will be working on the project, Project will calculate all the people-related costs for you.

Then you need to identify any external people costs, such as consultants, auditors, etc. and feed those in as well.

Finally identify any (non-people) material resource costs if your project is using costed material (such as paint or other types of consumables).

Fixed Costs

Once you have the internal and external, people and material resource costs, you then need to identify any internal non-staff costs, such as any one-off charges for the use of facilities, rooms, computer usage, etc.

Finally you will need to identify any other external capital or revenue costs, such as software package purchase, software development, equipment purchase or lease costs and any other items of external expenditure.

All of these costs can be input into Project as Resource Costs or Fixed Costs on an appropriate task.

We will now work through each of these cost types and use the remaining topics in this chapter to see how they are treated in Project.

Resource Costs

Costs can be applied to resources or tasks and typically you will use resource costs for people on the project. Resource costs are normally shown as an hourly rate that represents their salary plus overheads (that is their real cost to the business). Your organization may do things differently so follow whatever their procedure is to calculate the appropriate hourly rates. The easiest way to allocate costs to resources is in the Resource Sheet.

1 Open the Resource Sheet by selecting View>Resource Sheet from the Menu bar

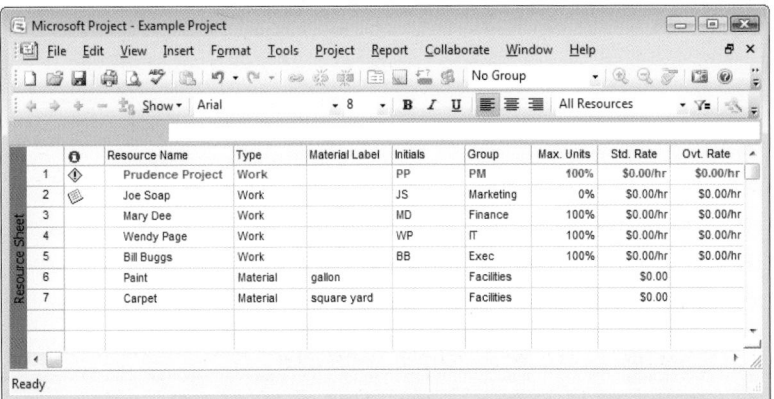

Hot tip

If any resources are highlighted in red it indicates a resource conflict (this is dealt with in chapter 11).

2 Enter the appropriate hourly standard rate (and overtime rate if appropriate) for each resource

		Resource Name	Type	Material Label	Initials	Group	Max. Units	Std. Rate	Ovt. Rate	Cost/Use
1		Prudence Project	Work		PP	PM	100%	$40.00/hr	$50.00/hr	$0.00
2		Joe Soap	Work		JS	Marketing	0%	$50.00/hr	$60.00/hr	$0.00
3		Mary Dee	Work		MD	Finance	100%	$30.00/hr	$35.00/hr	$0.00
4		Wendy Page	Work		WP	IT	100%	$35.00/hr	$40.00/hr	$0.00
5		Bill Buggs	Work		BB	Exec	100%	$60.00/hr	$60.00/hr	$0.00
6		Paint	Material	gallon		Facilities		$10.00		$0.00
7		Carpet	Material	square yard		Facilities		$17.50		$0.00
8		Travel & Expenses	Cost							

3 If a resource has a one-off cost for each use (such as hire of a meeting room) enter the cost in the Cost/Use field

4 Finally there is also a resource type of Cost (Travel & Expenses in the above example) which can be used to assign arbitrary costs to tasks

Fixed Costs

Fixed costs are used where a task has a fixed cost associated with it, rather than the cost being associated with the resource. In the following example we are going to add the cost of purchasing a software package to the task Purchase Package.

 In Gantt chart view select View>Table: Entry>Cost from the Menu bar. The cost columns will be added to the task table, replacing the task entry columns (as in the example below)

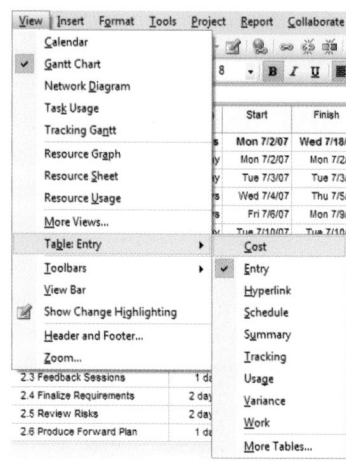

	Task Name	Fixed Cost	Fixed Cost Accrual	Total Cost
1	+ 1 Initiation Stage	$0.00	Prorated	$3,840.00
9	+ 2 Strategy Stage	$0.00	Prorated	$1,280.00
20	− 3 Analysis Stage	$0.00	Prorated	$14,800.00
21	3.1 Agree Requirements	$0.00	Prorated	$1,600.00
22	3.2 Select Package	$0.00	Prorated	$1,600.00
23	3.3 Purchase Package	$10,000.00	Prorated	$10,640.00
24	3.4 Contingency	$0.00	Prorated	$960.00
25	+ 4 Design & Build Stage	$0.00	Prorated	$0.00
27	+ 5 Implementation Stage	$0.00	Prorated	$0.00

2. Type the estimated fixed cost for the task into the Fixed Cost field

In this example there is also a resource allocated to the task and, therefore, the total cost of the task includes the fixed cost plus the resource cost (16 hours at $40 per hour). The other fields in the task cost table are baseline, actual, variance and remaining (see below).

	Task Name	Fixed Cost	Fixed Cost Accrual	Total Cost	Baseline	Variance	Actual	Remaining
1	+ 1 Initiation Stage	$0.00	Prorated	$3,840.00	$0.00	$3,840.00	$0.00	$3,840.00
9	+ 2 Strategy Stage	$0.00	Prorated	$1,280.00	$0.00	$1,280.00	$0.00	$1,280.00
20	− 3 Analysis Stage	$0.00	Prorated	$14,800.00	$0.00	$14,800.00	$0.00	$14,800.00
21	3.1 Agree Requirements	$0.00	Prorated	$1,600.00	$0.00	$1,600.00	$0.00	$1,600.00
22	3.2 Select Package	$0.00	Prorated	$1,600.00	$0.00	$1,600.00	$0.00	$1,600.00
23	3.3 Purchase Package	$10,000.00	Prorated	$10,640.00	$0.00	$10,640.00	$0.00	$10,640.00
24	3.4 Contingency	$0.00	Prorated	$960.00	$0.00	$960.00	$0.00	$960.00

Variable Resource Costs

It is quite possible that resource costs may change during the course of a project. For example, someone may receive a promotion or salary increase for doing such a good job on the project. Any changes to resource costs should be entered using the Resource Information dialog box.

1 In resource sheet view, select the Resource Name of the resource to be changed, click the Resource Information button on the toolbar to open the Resource Information dialog box and select the Costs tab

2 On the A (Default) tab, click in the next available Effective Date (below any existing cost information) and use the drop-down arrow to select the date for the new rate

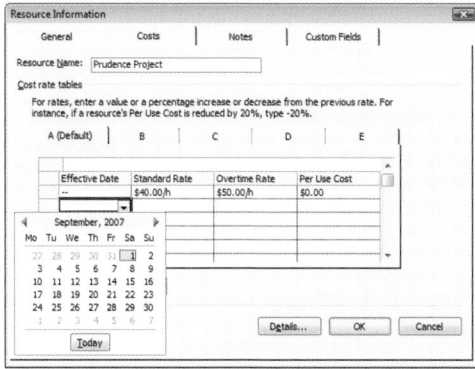

3 Then type in the new Standard Rate (and Overtime Rate if applicable) that will be effective from that date and click OK

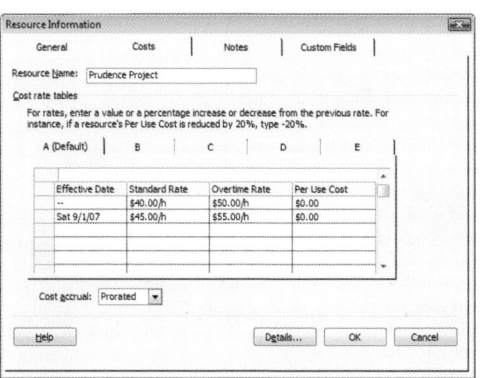

These new cost rates will become effective on all work from the effective date onwards. All work before that effective date will still be costed at the existing rate. If required, you can input up to 24 changes of resource costs for a resource.

Don't forget

You can also double-click on the Resource Name to open the Resource Information dialog box.

Hot tip

You can also put in a percentage figure for an increase or a negative percentage for a decrease.

Cost Rate Tables

In addition to being able to change cost rates, Project will also allow you to set up tables of rates for a resource. This can be useful if you need to use different cost rates for different types of work for the same person.

The cost rate tables are selected in the Costs tab in the Resource Information dialog box.

1 In resource sheet view double-click on a Resource Name to open the Resource Information dialog box

2 Select the Costs tab and then click on tab B in the Cost rate tables area

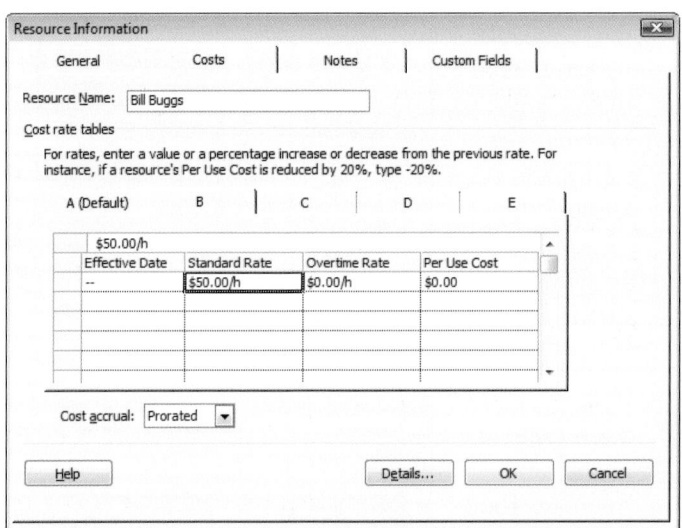

3 Type in the second standard rate (and overtime rate if required)

4 If required, rates can also be changed from effective dates as in the previous topic

5 You can select tab A (Default) to verify the original rate and add any other rates in tabs C, D and E if required

6 Click OK to save the new rates table

Applying Resource Rates

Having set up a cost rates table as in the previous topic, it can now be applied to any relevant tasks, where this resource is allocated. Rate A will be used by default unless it is changed.

1 Select View>Task Usage from the menu bar

	ⓘ	Task Name	Work	Duration	Details	Jul 2, '07 M	T	W	T	F	S
1		− Initiation Stage	80 hrs	13 days	Work	8h	8h	16h	16h	8h	
2		− Agree Project Objectives	8 hrs	1 day	Work	8h					
		Prudence Project	8 hrs		Work	8h					
3		− Identify Stakeholders	8 hrs	1 day	Work		8h				
		Prudence Project	8 hrs		Work		8h				
4		− Select Project Team	32 hrs	2 days	Work			16h	16h		
		Bill Buggs	16 hrs		Work			8h	8h		
		Prudence Project	16 hrs		Work			8h	8h		
5		− Identify Business Case	16 hrs	2 days	Work					8h	
		Prudence Project	16 hrs		Work					8h	

2 Identify the resource and task where you wish to apply a different rate and double-click on the Resource Name to open the Assignment Information dialog box

3 On the General tab, click on the down-arrow beside the Cost rate table to show the drop-down list of rates

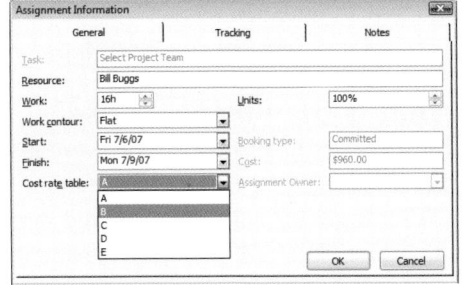

4 Select the rate you wish to apply to this task and click OK

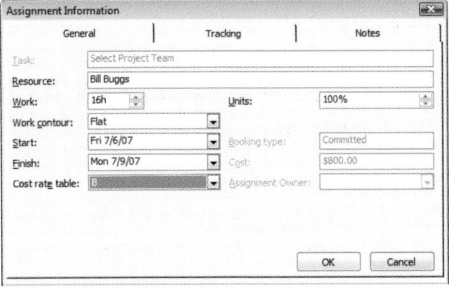

Note in the example above that the new cost rate has now been applied and the cost of the work on this task has been recalculated at the new rate. In the above example the cost of the 16 hours of work has changed from $960 to $800.

The Business Case

Once you have identified all the costs for the project, it is a good idea to re-examine the business case. The business case is the reason or justification for carrying out the project in the first place and once all the costs are known (or at least estimated), it may be that there is no longer a clear business case. If this is the situation the project should be reconsidered.

Who Owns the Business Case?

The project manager should not be responsible for making or supporting the business case. This is the responsibility of the project sponsor on behalf of the business. The project manager's role is to determine the real costs of the project so that the business can make the decision about the viability (or not) of the project.

The costs for a properly planned project will normally start fairly low and gradually build up through the life of the project. Planning should take place at the start of the project so that a reasonable idea of the likely cost is available before too much time and expenditure have taken place. Then if the decision is made to cancel the project, the costs of doing so will still be fairly low.

What is the Business Case?

The business case sets out the basic justification for the project. It therefore needs to include a statement of the expected costs of the project together with the expected benefits. For this reason it is sometimes referred to as a cost/benefit appraisal.

Project Costs

The costs of the project itself (and the costs of operating any new processes implemented as a result of it) should be set out over the expected life of the new process. The new process could be a new business or just a different way of working.

Project Benefits

The benefits (expressed over the same time period) should set out any expected savings as a result of the project plus any other quantifiable business benefits (e.g. new business revenue).

While the project manager should be responsible for the project costs, the benefits and the decision to go ahead with the project should be defined by the business or the project sponsor on behalf of the business.

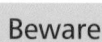

Beware

Make sure that the business owns the Business Case or you may end up being held accountable for it.

Risk Management

Risks are the things that could threaten your project, whether internal (something going wrong on the project itself) or external (something outside the project impacting it). If risks are not managed they are likely to have a disastrous effect on the project when they occur. This topic sets out a brief summary of a risk management process.

Risk Identification

The starting point is to identify all the risks that could impact your project. These could be straightforward like loosing a key resource at a critical time, or a sudden change in the business environment in which you operate. You should do this early in the project and involve the whole team.

Risk Estimation

Having identified the risks, each then needs to be rated on its probability (how likely it is to occur) and impact (how severely it will effect the project if it does occur). The simplest way is to rate each as Low, Medium or High.

Risk Evaluation

Based on the probability and impact, you then need to decide what can or should be done by way of countermeasures to mitigate the risk. This may involve steps to prevent or reduce the likelihood of the risk happening or it may involve pre-planning for how it will be dealt with if it does occur.

Risk Log

The essential step is to record all these risks, together with the impact and probability estimations and the planned countermeasures. These should be shared with the project sponsor and the business as they could well impact the business case.

Hot tip

Just recording details of project risks makes them less likely to happen.

Risk Reviews

Whether risk countermeasures are being taken or not (sometimes risks just have to be accepted) it is important to keep risks under review as the project proceeds. Over time risks will change. They may become more or less likely or their potential impact may get lesser or greater. Most important of all, however, is that new risks will probably arise during the course of the project. So regular risk reviews should be scheduled with the project team (ideally as part of a regular progress review) and with the project sponsor as part of a regular reporting process.

Summary

- Project costs need to be estimated early in the life of the project, but these early estimates should always be flagged as preliminary and liable to change

- If you have access to a finance department get them to help with the project costs

- In addition to the cost of the people working on the project, there may be other revenue (ongoing expenditure) costs and capital (purchase) costs

- In Project costs are either resource costs (costs associated with people or other resources) or fixed costs (which are not resource-related)

- Resource costs can be entered directly into the resource sheet view as hourly costs, material (quantity) costs or per use costs

- Fixed costs can be entered in Gantt chart view by applying the Cost table to the view

- Resource cost can be varied, to reflect changes in salary for example, by using the Costs tab in the Resource Information dialog box

- In addition to the default cost rate, four additional cost rates can be specified if a resource is to be charged differently for different types of work

- Non-default resource rates are best applied in the task usage view, through the Assignment Information dialog box

- The business case sets out the basic justification for carrying out the project. It should be owned by the business or project sponsor (on behalf of the business). It should include the full costs of the project together with the expected business benefits to be derived from carrying out the project

- Risk management is the process of identifying the risks to the project; estimating their likely probability and impact; evaluating what can or should be done about them; recording them in a risk log; and keeping them under review for the duration of the project

9 Project Calendars

This chapter explains what the various Project calendars are, how to create them, set them up for the project and assign and change them for individual resources.

Calendars

Scheduling a project consists of allocating tasks to resources in line with their availability. So, before you can start scheduling you need to know the availability and non-availability of the resources you will be using (e.g. if they are going to be on vacation or on a training course at any time during the project).

Project uses calendars to determine working and non-working days, default start time and the working hours in a day.

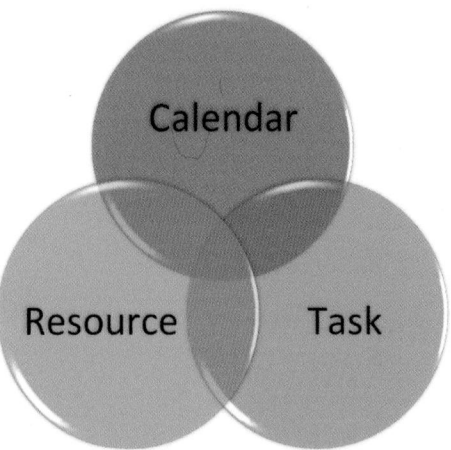

So resources, tasks and availability (the resource calendar) are all interlinked, as illustrated above. When you allocate a resource to a task, Project checks the resource calendar for their availability and if necessary reschedules the task to take account of the availability of the resource.

There are three types of calendar: base calendars, individual resource calendars and task calendars. Base calendars define the working days and hours for the whole project (or for a group of resources within the project). Resource calendars define the working days and working hours for each individual resource. Task calendars define when a task can or cannot take place.

The Standard calendar is the default project base calendar. It defines the working days and hours for the whole project.

When a resource is added to a project, the standard calendar is allocated to that resource as its base calendar. Any changes made to the standard calendar are reflected in the resource calendars that are based on it.

There is a third element to this relationship and that is the project defaults. These form the top-level of the relationship, as illustrated:

1 The Options dialog box allows you to change the default working hours, hours in a working day, hours in a working week and even days in a working month. These are all used by Project in setting task durations and allocating resources to tasks

Beware

Making any changes to these defaults can have a significant impact on your project schedule. This is covered in the next topic.

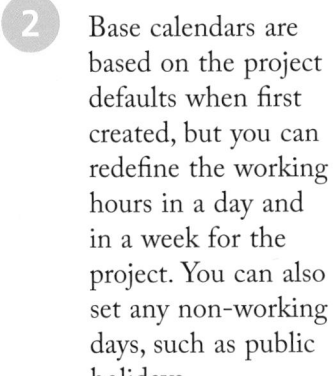

2 Base calendars are based on the project defaults when first created, but you can redefine the working hours in a day and in a week for the project. You can also set any non-working days, such as public holidays

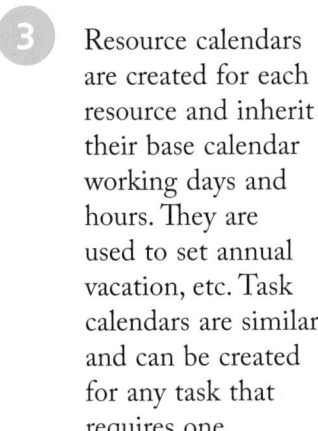

3 Resource calendars are created for each resource and inherit their base calendar working days and hours. They are used to set annual vacation, etc. Task calendars are similar and can be created for any task that requires one

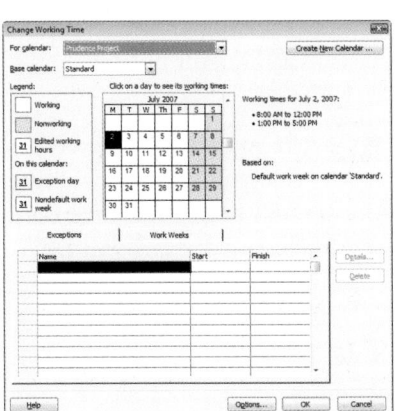

Project Defaults

Beware

Even if you don't work these hours, don't change the defaults unless you absolutely have to. It can make scheduling a real nightmare.

Project defaults are initially set so that working time is Monday to Friday, 8:00 AM to 12:00 PM and 1:00 PM to 5:00 PM. The standard calendar (see next topic) is also initially set to these working days and times.

Changing the defaults will change the way that tasks are allocated, duration and the way that resources are allocated to tasks. If you change the project defaults it does not automatically change the standard calendar or any calendars based on it. So if you do make changes to the defaults you may also need to make changes to all your other calendars.

1 Select Tools>Options from the Menu bar

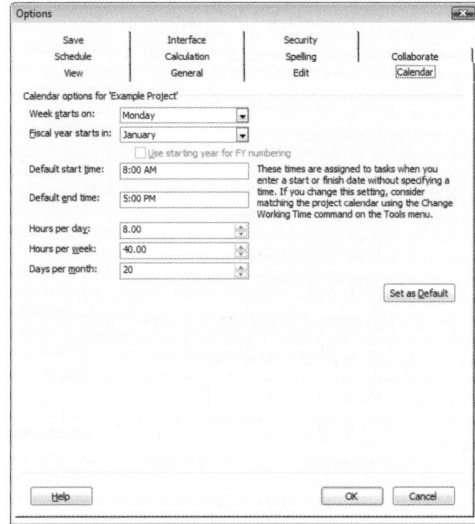

2 Click on the Calendar tab to open the project defaults

3 Make any changes required to the project defaults and click OK

4 If you want these changes to apply to all future projects that you create, as well as the current one, click on the Set as Default button

Beware

If you change the Default hours per day after you have entered any tasks, the task durations will change as they will still have the original hours as their work effort.

5 If you have made any changes to the Default start time, Default end time, Hours per day or Hours per week, you will need to change the Standard calendar (and any other base calendars you have created) to bring it in line with the new defaults (see next topic)

Note: If you are going to change the defaults you should do so before entering any tasks or resources (see the warning on left).

Standard Calendar

The standard calendar has the default working time set as 8:00 AM to 12:00 PM and 1:00 PM to 5:00 PM on Monday to Friday. You need to set it up for your project by making any changes to the working hours and then putting in any public or other holidays that will apply to the whole project.

1 Select Tools>Change Working Time from the Menu bar to open the Change Working Time dialog box

2 The scroll bar on the right of the calendar changes the month. Click on a day to show its working time

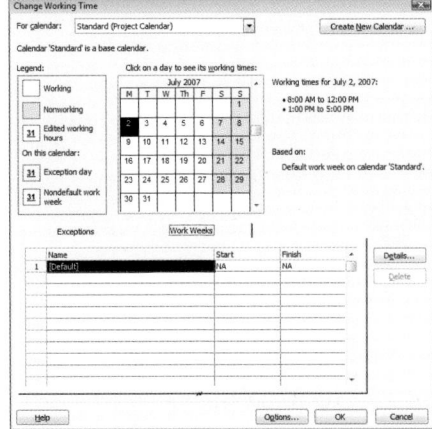

Beware

In versions before Project 2007, calendars will look different and changes to working time are made directly in the Change Working Time dialog box.

111

3 To change all working times select the Work Weeks tab, select Default and click the Details button

4 In the Details dialog box, select the days to change (Monday to Friday for the whole week), change the From times and To times as required and click OK

5 To enter holidays, select the required month and day, click the Exceptions tab, enter the holiday name and click the Details button

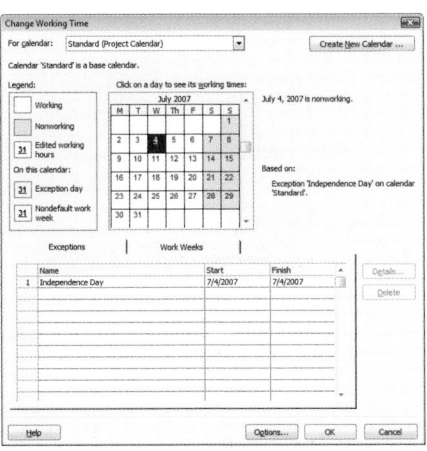

6 In the Details dialog box make the day non-working and click OK to save it

New Base Calendar

Project comes with three base calendars (standard, night shift and 24 hours) but if none of these are suitable, you can create a new one from the project defaults or by copying an existing calendar.

1 Open the Change Working Time dialog box and click Create New Calendar (in the top right-hand corner)

2 Name the new calendar and select if you want to start with a copy of an existing calendar

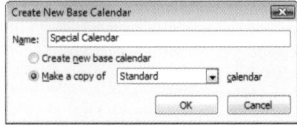

The new calendar will open in the Change Working Time dialog box and will inherit anything from the calendar you based it on.

3 Select the Work Weeks tab, select Default, click on the Details button to open the Details dialog box and enter details of your required working time

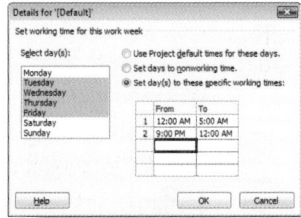

This example is for a shift so Monday would need to be 9:00 PM to 12:00 AM and Saturday 12:00 AM to 5:00 AM.

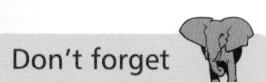

Don't forget

In Project 12:00 AM is midnight and 12:00 PM is midday. If you select the 24-hour clock 00:00 is midnight and 12:00 is midday.

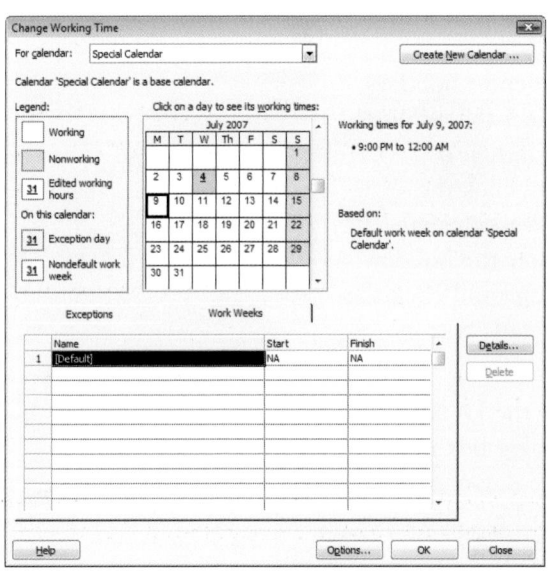

Assigning a Calendar

Having set up your standard calendar and created any new base calendars you require, you can now assign them to the project team as required. The standard calendar is assigned by default and the other base calendars can be assigned using the Resource Information dialog box or directly in Resource Sheet view.

Hot tip

If you have made changes to a resource calendar and then assign a new base calendar to the resource, the changes will be retained and applied to the new base calendar.

1. Double-click on the Resource Name, of the person you want to assign a new base calendar, to open the Resource Information dialog box

2. On the General tab click the Change Working Time button (on the right) to open the Change Working Time dialog box for the resource

3. Click the down arrow beside Base calendar to get the drop down list of calendars, select the required base calendar and click OK. Click OK again to close the Resource Information dialog box

4. To assign a new base calendar directly in Resource Sheet view, click on the existing Base Calendar (on the right-hand side of the sheet) and select the required calendar from the drop down list

Resource Name	Type	Material Label	Initials	Group	Max. Units	Std. Rate	Ovt. Rate	Cost/Use	Accrue At	Base Calendar
Joe Soap	Work		JS	Marketing	0%	$50.00/hr	$60.00/hr	$0.00	Prorated	Standard
Mary Dee	Work		MD	Finance	100%	$30.00/hr	$35.00/hr	$0.00	Prorated	Standard
Wendy Page	Work		WP	IT	100%	$35.00/hr	$40.00/hr	$0.00	Prorated	Standard
Bill Buggs	Work		BB	Exec	100%	$60.00/hr	$60.00/hr	$0.00	Prora	24 Hours
Paint	Material	gallon		Facilities		$10.00		$0.00	Prora	Night Shift
Carpet	Material	square yard		Facilities		$17.50		$0.00	Prora	Special Calendar
Travel & Expenses	Cost								Prora	Standard

The new base calendar is applied to the resource in exactly the same way as using the Resource Information dialog box.

Task Calendar

Task Calendars are not available in versions before Project 2000.

If a task can only take place at a certain time and/or on certain days, this can be defined by assigning a task calendar to the task.

For example it may be that a presentation to management must take place at a weekly management meeting and these are always held on Friday mornings.

1 First we need to split the task into the report preparation and the presentation (to isolate the presentation)

	ⓘ	Task Name	Duration	Start
15		2.4 Finalize Requirements	2 days	Wed 8/1/07
16		2.5 Review Risks	2 days	Fri 8/3/07
17		2.6 Produce Forward Plan	1 day	Tue 8/7/07
18		− 2.7 Report to Management	2 days	Wed 8/8/07
19		2.7.1 Prepare Report	1.5 days	Wed 8/8/07
20		2.7.2 Present to Management	0.5 days	Thu 8/9/07
21		2.8 Contingency	6 days	Fri 8/10/07

114

By making a copy of a standard calendar it will inherit any holidays.

2 Create a new base Management Meeting calendar (as a copy of Standard) and click OK

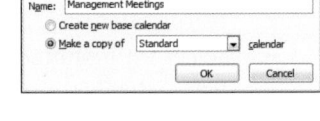

3 The change working time dialog box will open at the new calendar. Select Default on the Work Weeks tab and click the Details button

4 Select Monday to Thursday on the left, then click on the Set days to non-working time button on the right

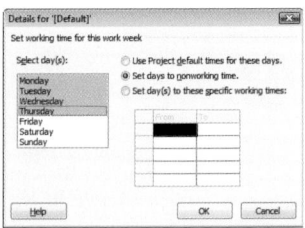

5 Then select Friday on the left and delete the afternoon From working time (this will also delete the afternoon To working time) to just leave Friday mornings as working time

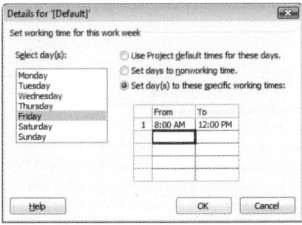

6 Click OK to save this

We have now created the Management Meetings calendar with just Friday mornings as working time. We now have to assign it to the relevant task as a task calendar.

 7 In Gantt chart view, double-click on the Present to Management task to open the Task Information dialog box

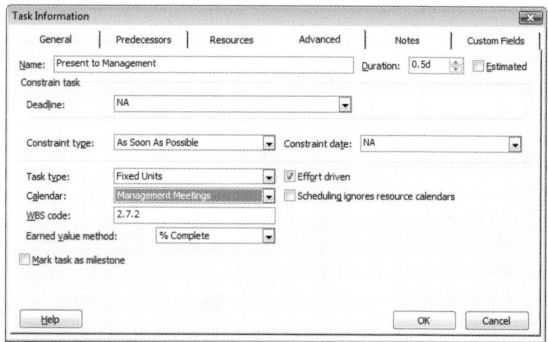

 8 On the Advanced tab, assign the new calendar and the task is rescheduled to the next available Friday morning (as below)

	❶	Task Name	Duration	Start	Aug 6, '07 S M T W T F S S	Aug 13, '07 M T W T F S
15		2.4 Finalize Requirements	2 days	Wed 8/1/07		
16		2.5 Review Risks	2 days	Fri 8/3/07		
17		2.6 Produce Forward Plan	1 day	Tue 8/7/07		
18		– 2.7 Report to Management	2.5 days	Wed 8/8/07		
19		2.7.1 Prepare Report	1.5 days	Wed 8/8/07		
20		2.7.2 Present to Management	0.5 days	Fri 8/10/07		
21		2.8 Contingency	6 days	Fri 8/10/07		

As the delay to the presentation to management has effectively put a 1 day lag time between preparing the report and presenting it to management, the tasks in front of it are no longer on the critical path (note that they have turned blue). They can slip by 1 day without impacting the project. Of course the end of the project has just been put back by 1 day as well (unless there is spare lag time further on in the project).

One final point to note is a task calendar symbol has now been created in the task information box to warn us that this task has a calendar assigned to it.

115

Resource Calendar

Each resource is automatically assigned a resource calendar. This is initially based on the standard calendar, although a different base calendar can be assigned. The resource calendar will inherit any holidays or project-wide variations but it also needs to have resource-specific variations added, such as vacation or other non-working time.

1 In Resource Sheet view, double-click on the resource you wish to change to open the Resource Information dialog box and on the General tab, click the Change Working Time button

2 Select the day where you want the vacation (or non-working time) to start, click under Name on the Exception tab, type in a description for the non-working time and press Tab. The Start date will be inserted

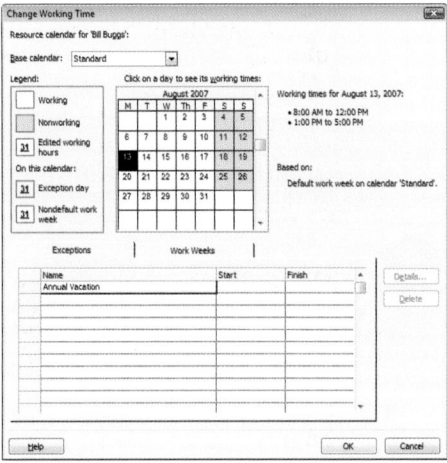

3 Click in the Finish date box and use the drop down calendar to select the required finish date. Click OK twice to save the changes and close the resource information dialog box

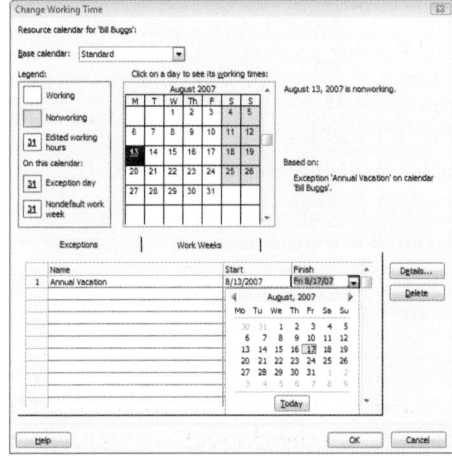

Communication Plan

Building up the project and resource calendars involves communication with the people who will be doing the work on the project. These are obviously a key group of stakeholders, but they are not the only stakeholders and all stakeholders will need some form of communication during the project. The best way of ensuring that this happens is to produce a communication plan.

1   First make sure you have a full list of all your project stakeholders. You may have done this as part of your project start up, but if not now is a good time to do it

2   Having listed all your project stakeholders, try to identify their vested interest in the project (what they want to get out of it)

3   Now, based on their interest in the project, you should be able to identify what information you will need to communicate to them to keep them happy

4   Now that you have identified what you are going to communicate to each of your stakeholders (or groups of stakeholders), you need to identify how you are going to communicate it

Communication Methods

Communication by email seems to be the default these days but it is not necessarily the most effective means of communication. Many projects are starting to use Web Logs (blogs) to keep their stakeholders informed. That way they can choose how much or how little they read. However if something is important, it is worth considering that people are said to remember:

10% of what they read

20% of what they hear

30% of what they see

50% of what they see and hear

So if a piece of information is important enough consider communicating through a presentation for maximum impact.

Hot tip

However you choose to communicate, keep on doing it, don't stop.

Summary

- When allocating a resource to a task and scheduling it, Project uses calendars to check the availability of that resource to carry out the task and any limitations on when the task can be performed

- Project defaults determine how Project will schedule work, base calendars are used to define project or group working times and resource calendars are used to determine an individual resource's availability. Task calendars provide an option for determining when a task can be performed

- Project defaults specify the number of working hours in a day and a week, for scheduling purposes, and the default start and end time for a working day. They also define the first day of the week, the start of the fiscal year and the number of working days in a month

- The standard (project) calendar is the default base calendar for the project and is where project working time and non-working days are specified. It needs to be kept in step with the project defaults

- A new base calendar is best created based on the standard calendar so that it inherits any project information

- The standard calendar is allocated to all resources by default but any other base calendar can be allocated through the change working time dialog box or on the resource sheet

- Task calendars are used when a task can only happen at certain times. They are defined by limiting the working time and then allocated to a task through the task information dialog box

- Resource calendars are used to set the non-working time for each individual resource by defining their vacations and other non-available times

- All the project resources and other stakeholders will need to be communicated with during the project. Producing a communication plan will make this an effective process and ensure it continues to happen

10 Project Scheduling

This chapter deals with scheduling a project and how the different task types and contouring effect that process.

Scheduling

The process of scheduling uses the tasks, the resources allocated to them and the resource and task calendars to work out when tasks can be started, worked on and completed.

Forward-Scheduling

The default approach to scheduling is to forward-schedule from a start date. You can also backward-schedule from a finish date although there are certain problems that can result from this (covered later in this chapter).

The way that the schedule will be affected when resources, work effort or durations change is also dependent on the scheduling method and task types. The scheduling method can be either effort-driven or not. Tasks can be of fixed unit, fixed duration or fixed work types. The default is fixed unit, effort-driven but we will look at examples of each of these types.

Effort-Driven Scheduling

This is the default scheduling method in Project. In this method the duration of a task is adjusted to fit in with any changes to the resources. If a task is going to require 16 hours' work effort and you allocate two resources to it (at 100%), it will be given a duration of 8 hours or 1 day.

If you then remove one of the resources, the additional day's work will be reallocated to the remaining resource and so the duration will be extended to 2 days.

You can turn effort-driven scheduling off for a specific task or for all new tasks. When effort-driven scheduling is turned off, adding an additional resource to a 2 day duration, fixed unit task will increase the work effort by 2 days to 4 days, but the duration will remain unchanged (as there are now two people doing it).

Task Types

The task type (fixed unit, fixed duration or fixed work) will determine what will be changed to accommodate any other changes. The basic equation used by Project is:

$$Work = Duration \times Units$$

Where Work is the work effort required, Duration is how long it will take and Units are resources and their percentage allocation.

Fixed Unit Tasks

The fixed unit task is the default task type in Project. If resources are added to or removed from a task, the duration will usually be affected. In the following example we will allocate first one and then a second resource to a task.

1 In Gantt chart view select View>More Views from the Menu bar, then select Task Entry and click the Apply button

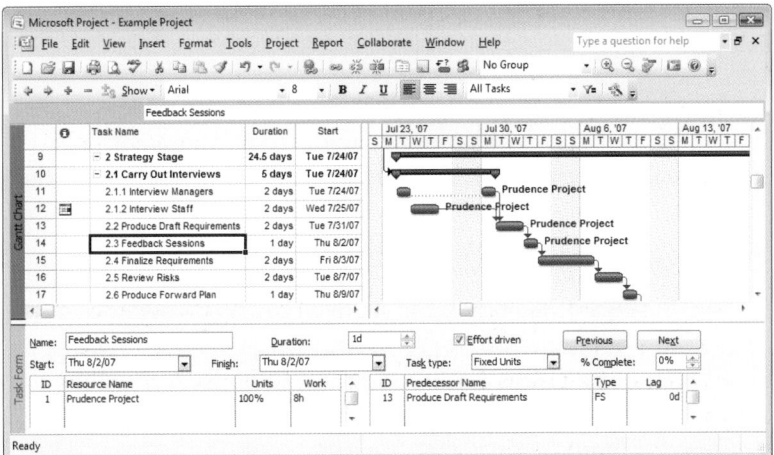

2 In the above example, we have selected a 1 day task and assigned a single resource to it. Note that the duration rcmains at 1 day and that 8 hours of work have been allocated to the resource in the (lower) task form

3 If we now assign a second resource to the task (note below) that the duration has been reduced to half a day with 4 hours work allocated to each of the two resources. This task type is suitable where you want to alter the duration by assigning more or less resources

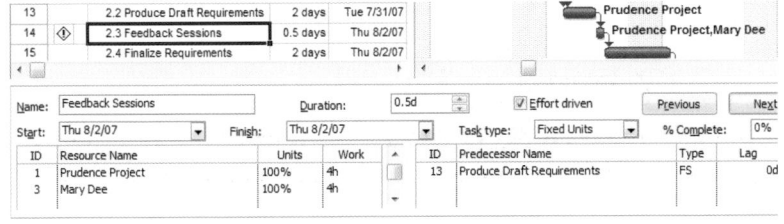

Hot tip

Note the smart tag in the task information box. This allows you to override the rescheduling by increasing the total work or reducing the hours worked.

Fixed Duration Tasks

If a task is a fixed duration task, then (as the name implies) the duration remains fixed whether resources are added or removed. This has an impact on the way scheduling takes place, depending on whether effort-driven scheduling is being used or not.

Effort-Driven Scheduling

If effort-driven scheduling is being used this means that adding another resource to an existing task will split the work between the two resources. The effort will remain the same, the duration will remain the same so their units will be reduced to 50% to balance.

Non-Effort-Driven Scheduling

If effort-driven scheduling is not being used this means that adding another resource to an existing task will double the work. The duration stays the same, the units will be 100%, so the work effort will double (an example of this follows).

1 Select a 1 day task with one resource allocated to it and, in the lower panel (task form), change the task type to Fixed Duration and deselect "Effort driven"

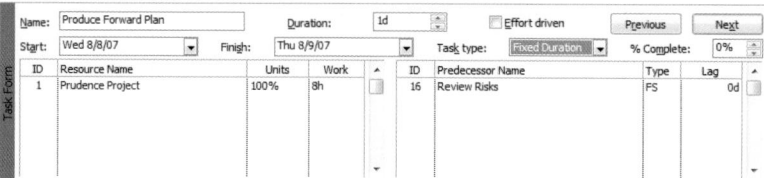

2 Now if a second resource is assigned to the task

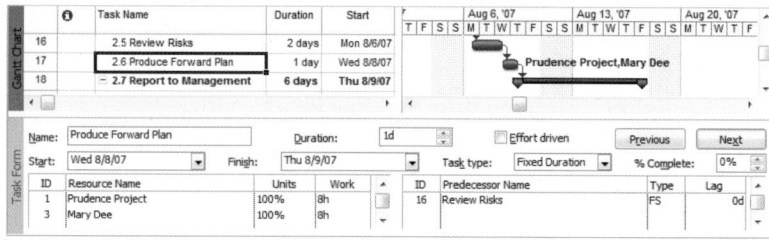

The duration has stayed the same so the work has doubled to 16 hours. This is the type of task to use where duration stays the same regardless of the number of resources allocated.

Fixed Work Tasks

The third type of task is the fixed work task. A fixed work task must be effort-driven (as the amount of work is fixed) so only the duration and resource units can be affected. Adding another resource will reduce the duration while increasing the duration will reduce the resource units (an example of this follows).

1 Select a task with one resource assigned to it and, in the lower panel (task form), change the Task type to Fixed Work (note that "Effort driven" deselects so it cannot be changed) and click OK

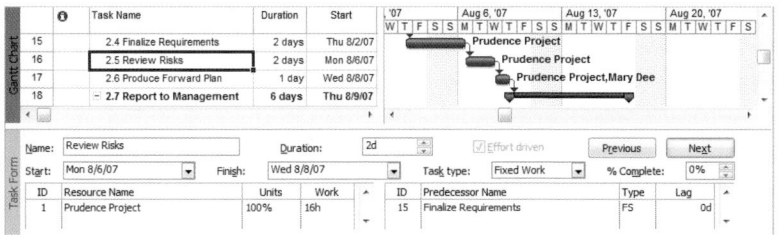

2 Now if a second resource is assigned to the task, note (below) that the work effort remains 16 hours so the duration has reduced to 1 day

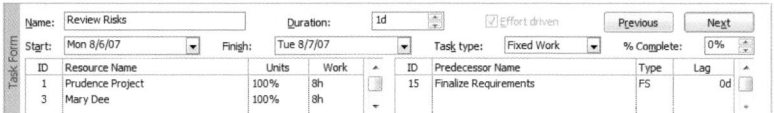

3 Change the Duration back to 2 days and the resource units are reduced to 50% so work stays at 16 hours

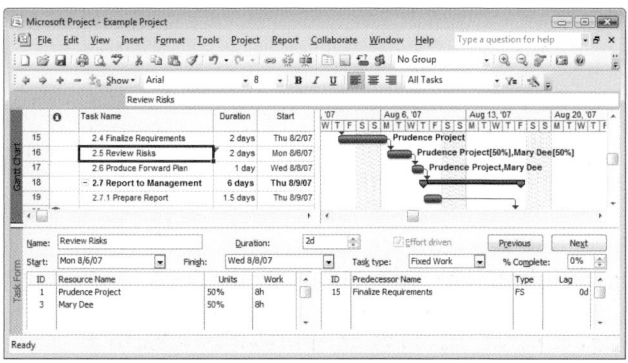

Contouring

When you assign a resource to a task, the total work is spread evenly throughout the duration of the task. This is referred to as a flat contour but there are a number of other contours that you can apply in Project.

Contours can be applied or changed in Task Usage or Resource Usage views. In the former, the resources are grouped by task; in the latter, tasks are grouped by resource. In both cases the right-hand side of the screen displays the work values and is used to contour the work.

Contours are applied using the Assignment Information dialog box. There are eight preset contours available:

Flat
Work hours are distributed evenly through the task duration.

Back Loaded
The hours start low and ramp up towards the end of the task.

Front Loaded
The hours start at 100% at the start of the task and tail off towards the end.

Double Peak
The hours peak twice during the task duration.

Early Peak
The hours peak during the first quarter of the task duration.

Late Peak
The hours peak during the last quarter of the task duration.

Bell
The hours start and finish low and peak in the middle of the task duration.

Turtle
Similar to Bell but the hours start and finish higher (i.e. there is less variation).

Once a contour has been applied to a task, any changes to the task start or finish dates, the resources allocated or the duration will be applied using that contour.

Applying a Contour

We will now look at applying a contour in Resource Usage view (the process is the same in Task Usage view).

1 In Resource Usage view, select a task that is at least 2 days long (contouring is only really practical on larger tasks)

	ⓘ	Resource Name	Work	Details	Jul 2, '07 M	T	W	T	F	S	S	Jul 9, '07 M	T	W
1		− Prudence Project	268 hrs	Work	8h	8h		8h	8h			8h	8h	
		Agree Project Objectives	8 hrs	Work	8h									
		Identify Stakeholders	8 hrs	Work		8h								
		Select Project Team	16 hrs	Work				8h	8h					
		Identify Business Case	16 hrs	Work								8h	8h	
		Analyze the Risks	8 hrs	Work										
		Produce Outline Project Plan	8 hrs	Work										
	✍	Interview Managers	16 hrs	Work										
		Interview Staff	16 hrs	Work										

2 Double-click on the task to open the Assignment Information dialog box and select the General tab (if not already selected)

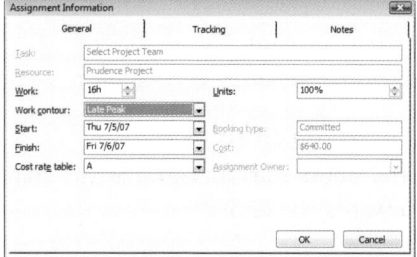

3 Click the down arrow beside Work contour, select the contour you wish to apply and click OK (in the example above Late Peak was selected)

	ⓘ	Resource Name	Work	Details	Jul 2, '07 M	T	W	T	F	S	S	Jul 9, '07 M	T	W
1		− Prudence Project	268 hrs	Work	8h	8h		1.2h	3.6h			7.2h	4h	8h
		Agree Project Objectives	8 hrs	Work	8h									
		Identify Stakeholders	8 hrs	Work		8h								
	⩗	Select Project Team	16 hrs	Work				1.2h	3.6h			7.2h	4h	
		Identify Business Case	16 hrs	Work										8h
		Analyze the Risks	8 hrs	Work										
		Produce Outline Project Plan	8 hrs	Work										
	✍	Interview Managers	16 hrs	Work										
		Interview Staff	16 hrs	Work										

The 16 hours work in the example above has now been contoured so that the hours build up slowly and peak late in the task. The larger the task the more apparent the contouring will be. The late peak symbol has been inserted into the task information box to indicate that a contour has been applied to the task.

Try applying the other contour types to see their effects on a task.

125

Resource Contouring

Project includes a feature that allows you to contour resource availability. This feature is aimed at situations where an individual is only available to a project part-time, with the percentage of their time available changing from period to period. Alternatively, it would be applicable if a team of people were going to be working on a task or set of tasks and the team were going to have varying numbers of people available over time (perhaps building up the team initially and then releasing them in a phased way).

Applying a resource contour is quite straightforward:

1 In Resource Sheet view, open the Resource Information dialog box for the resource you wish to contour, by double-clicking the Resource Name

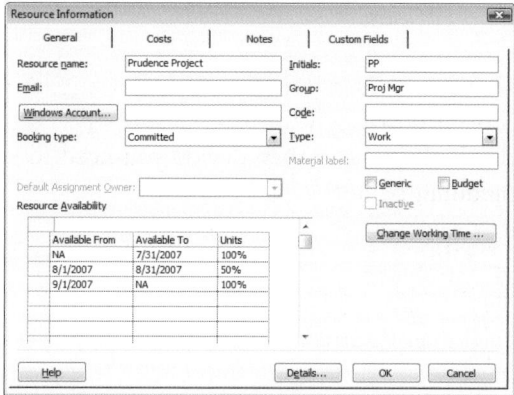

2 Enter the Available From and Available To dates with the relevant Units (in the above example the resource is only available 50% during August)

3 If this produces any conflicts with the scheduled work for this resource, the resource will be highlighted in red with a warning symbol in the Resource Information box (see below). Conflicts are dealt with in the next chapter.

	❶	Resource Name	Type	Material Label	Initials	Group	Max. Units
1	⬥	Prudence Project	Work		PP	Proj Mgr	100%
2		⬥ This resource should be leveled based on a Day by Day setting.			JS	Marketing	0%
3					MD	Finance	100%

Backward-Scheduling

The default method of scheduling is forward-scheduling from the project start date. This is what we have been using in all the examples so far. However, there may be times when you have to complete a project by a certain date. By scheduling backwards from a finish date, you can see when a project has to start. However, there is a right and a wrong way to go about this.

The Right Way

Use backward-scheduling right from the start. When you first create your project set it to schedule back from the required completion date before you input any tasks:

1. Create a new project and select Project>Project Information from the Menu bar. Select Schedule from: Project Finish Date, enter the required finish date for the project and click OK

Then as you input your tasks and allocate resources, Project will correctly backward-schedule your project. But what if you start off with forward-scheduling and then decide you need to switch to backward-scheduling?

The Wrong Way

Project will allow you to change from forward- to backward-scheduling but it doesn't always work. So save your project file before trying this.

1. Open your project in Gantt chart view, select Show Outline Level 1 and zoom out to get the whole project into view

2. Select Project>Project Information from the Menu bar, change Schedule from: to Project Finish Date, enter the required finish date and click OK

3. Accept any warnings and carry on until the project has been rescheduled

Sometimes this works and sometimes it doesn't. If it worked save the project with a new name. If it didn't work you may have to start again by creating a new project (the right way).

Beware

Scheduling back from a finish date is more difficult and should be avoided until you have some experience of forward-scheduling.

Summary

- Scheduling involves Project taking the tasks, the resources allocated to them and the resource calendars to work out the best time for each task to start and finish

- Work is the effort that will be required to complete a task (usually expressed in hours), duration is the length of time it will actually take (usually measured in days), and units are the resources that will be used to complete a task (expressed as a percentage, where 100% = one full resource)

- Effort-driven scheduling is the default and this means that duration is adjusted to accommodate any changes in resources

- The basic equation used by Project in scheduling tasks is Work = Duration x Units

- Fixed unit tasks are the default, where the units (resource percentage) remain constant and duration changes according to the number of resources allocated

- Fixed duration tasks with effort-driven scheduling will split the work between the resources if more resources are added

- Fixed duration tasks with non-effort-driven scheduling will increase the work if more resources are added

- Fixed work tasks will only adjust duration and resource units, so adding a resource will reduce the resource percentage

- After a change, you can over-ride the way Project has rescheduled using the smart tag in the task information box

- Contouring is the process of ramping work on a task up and down and there are seven contour profiles that can be applied in addition to flat (the default)

- Resource contouring is the process of applying a different availability (unit percentage) over a series of time periods

- Backward-scheduling is an option in Project but, if it is to be used, it should be used from the start of the project. While a forward-scheduled project can be changed to backward-scheduling, the results are not always predictable and it is best avoided if possible

11 Conflicts and Constraints

This chapter deals with resource conflicts and using leveling to resolve them. It also introduces task constraints, baselines and interim plans.

Resource Conflicts

As you begin to assign resources to tasks and then make subsequent changes to tasks and schedules, you will begin to get resource conflicts.

A resource conflict is where a resource is scheduled to perform more work than it can carry out in the time available. Project flags these conflicts for you by highlighting the relevant resource information in red and displaying a leveling indicator. Once these conflicts are identified the schedule needs to be examined and a decision made on how to resolve the conflict.

You can resolve these conflicts manually using Project scheduling or you can let Project automatically adjust the schedule by changing resources or task assignments for you. As an example we will create a resource conflict:

1   Select Tools>Level Resources from the Menu bar and make sure leveling is set to Manual (the default)

		Task Name	Duration	Start	Jul 23, '07 S M T W T F S S	Jul 30, '07 M T W T F S
10		− 2.1 Carry Out Interviews	5 days	Wed 7/25/07		
11		2.1.1 Interview Managers	2 days	Wed 7/25/07		Prudence
12		2.1.2 Interview Staff	2 days	Thu 7/26/07	Prudence Project	
13		2.2 Produce Draft Requirements	2 days	Wed 8/1/07		Prud
14		2.3 Feedback Sessions	0.5 days	Fri 8/3/07		Pru

2   In the example above, we will drag task 2.1.2 Interview Staff back to start 1 day earlier

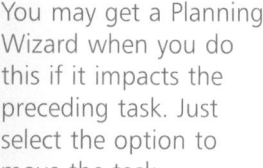

		Task Name	Duration	Start	Jul 23, '07 S M T W T F S S	Jul 30, '07 M T W T F S
10		− 2.1 Carry Out Interviews	5 days	Wed 7/25/07		
11		2.1.1 Interview Managers	2 days	Wed 7/25/07		Prudence
12		2.1.2 Interview Staff	2 days	Wed 7/25/07	Prudence Project	
13		2.2 Produce Draft Requirements	2 days	Wed 8/1/07		Prud
14		2.3 Feedback Sessions	0.5 days	Fri 8/3/07		Pru

As there are now two overlapping tasks allocated to the same resource, we have created a resource conflict. Effectively we are asking the resource to perform 16 hours work on Wednesday but there is nothing to indicate this in the Gantt chart view.

3   Select View>Resource Usage from the Menu bar to display the resource usage

In resource usage view (and other resource views), overallocated resources will be highlighted in red as will days on which overallocation occurs, scroll to the relevant tasks as illustrated below.

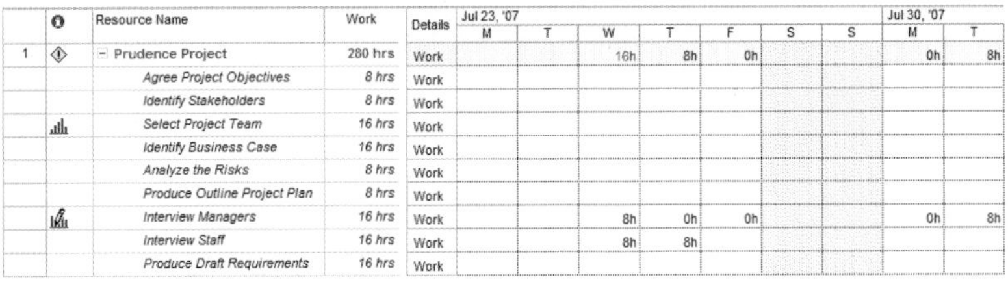

		Resource Name	Work	Details	Jul 23, '07 M	T	W	T	F	S	S	Jul 30, '07 M	T
1		− Prudence Project	280 hrs	Work			16h	8h	0h			0h	8h
		Agree Project Objectives	8 hrs	Work									
		Identify Stakeholders	8 hrs	Work									
		Select Project Team	16 hrs	Work									
		Identify Business Case	16 hrs	Work									
		Analyze the Risks	8 hrs	Work									
		Produce Outline Project Plan	8 hrs	Work									
		Interview Managers	16 hrs	Work			8h	0h	0h			0h	8h
		Interview Staff	16 hrs	Work			8h	8h					
		Produce Draft Requirements	16 hrs	Work									

In the example above, note that the resource name on the summary line is highlighted in red, together with the Wednesday on which we created the overallocation of 16 hours. The details of the task are shown below the summary line so that you can see exactly which tasks have caused the problem. There are some useful options we can use in investigating resource conflicts.

4. Select View>Toolbars>Resource Management from the Menu bar to open the Resource Management toolbar

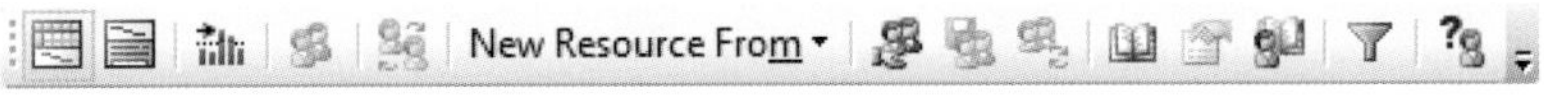

5. Click on the Resource Allocation button (far left above) to open the resource allocation view

6. The Go To Next Overallocation button (third from left, above) will bring the next overallocation into view

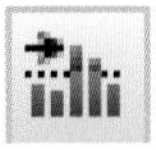

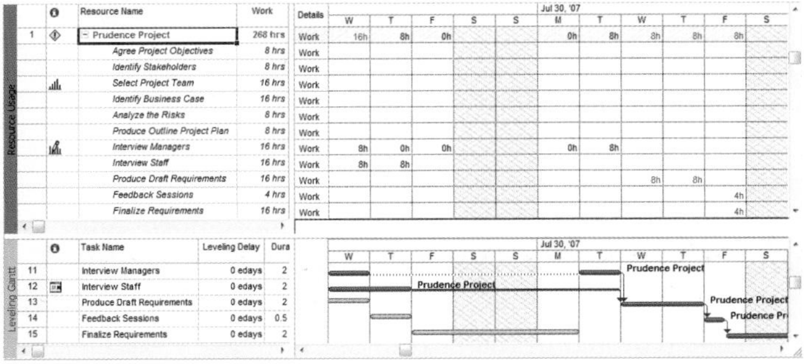

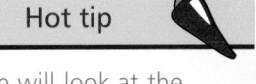

Hot tip

We will look at the options for resolving these overallocations in the next two topics.

Resource Leveling

In Project, resource conflicts can be resolved either manually or automatically. The process used to resolve these conflicts is called resource leveling.

Hot tip

Always save your project before leveling, then if anything goes wrong, you can always get back to where you were.

 Select View>More Views>Resource Allocation view from the Menu bar and click the Apply button

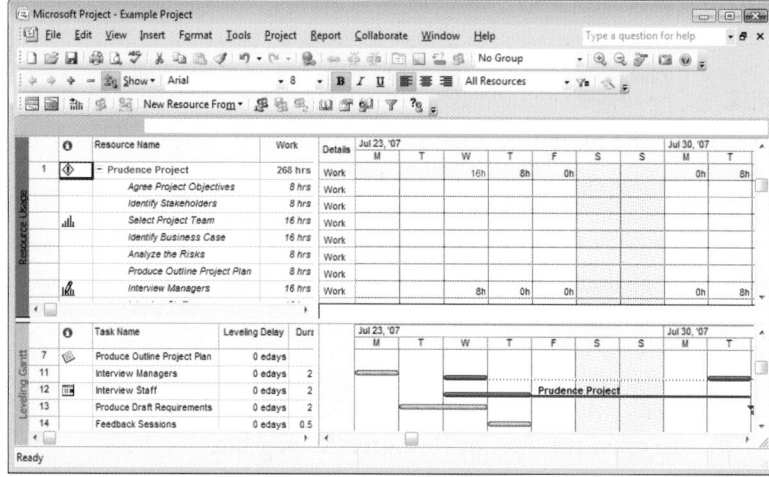

132

Hot tip

If you select automatic leveling, Project will prevent any resource conflicts occurring.

Select Project>Project Information from the Menu bar and note the current project finish date

Select the lower (Leveling Gantt) panel so that it is active

Select Tools>Level Resources from the Menu bar to open the Resource Leveling dialog box

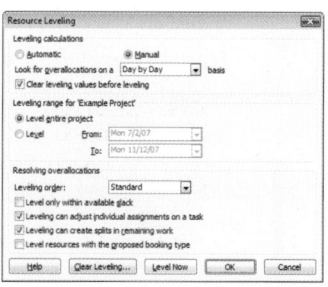

Check that leveling is set to manual and click the Level Now button

You may receive warnings that Project cannot resolve some over-allocations. If so make a note of the dates and click on the Skip button to continue. You will need to deal with these using manual adjustments (covered in the next topic).

Resource Leveling Issues

There are some issues with Project when carrying out resource leveling. In the example we have been using we allocated our project manager to a task (2.2 Produce Draft Requirements) at 100% so the 2 days work was scheduled as 2 days duration.

We then reduced the project manager's availability to 50% for August (on page 126), but it did not change the schedule (causing an overallocation). Now we have performed resource leveling, but Project cannot cope with this. It has scheduled the first day on July 31 (100% available) but then split the task and scheduled the second day on September 03 (when the resource is available 100% again). This is clearly not right but we can fix it.

	Task Name	Duration	Start
10	− 2.1 Carry Out Interviews	5 days	Tue 7/24/07
11	2.1.1 Interview Managers	2 days	Tue 7/24/07
12	2.1.2 Interview Staff	2 days	Wed 7/25/07
13	2.2 Produce Draft Requirements	2 days	Tue 7/31/07
14	2.3 Feedback Sessions	0.5 days	Tue 9/4/07
15	2.4 Finalize Requirements	2 days	Tue 9/4/07

1 Select the task and click on the Assign Resources button to open the Assign Resources dialog box

2 Select the resource and click the Remove button

3 Then select the same resource, click the Assign button and then reduce the Units to 50%

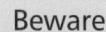

	❶	Task Name	Duration	Start
10		− 2.1 Carry Out Interviews	5 days	Tue 7/24/07
11		2.1.1 Interview Managers	2 days	Tue 7/24/07
12		2.1.2 Interview Staff	2 days	Wed 7/25/07
13		2.2 Produce Draft Requirements	4 days	Tue 7/31/07
14		2.3 Feedback Sessions	0.5 days	Mon 8/6/07
15		2.4 Finalize Requirements	2 days	Mon 8/6/07

The task has now been rescheduled to take 4 days duration at 50% and finish on August 03. This means the resource has only been allocated at 50% on July 31 (when they are actually available 100%) but it is the easiest way to deal with this issue.

Beware

This is a known issue and can be avoided if tasks are only allocated at a single rate of availability.

133

Manual Adjustments

In addition to using resource leveling to automatically resolve resource conflicts, you will also need to resolve some conflicts manually. This may be necessary if you do not want Project to extend the schedule, or (as in the previous topic) where Project cannot resolve the conflict.

Resolving a conflict manually can involve a number of options:

- Allocating more resources to a task

- Rescheduling or splitting a task

- Reallocating tasks to a different resource

- Adding overtime working

We will look at each of these in turn.

Allocating More Resources
To add additional resources to a task select the task and click on the Assign Resources button (see Fixed Unit Tasks on page 121 for an example).

Rescheduling a Task
The easiest way to reschedule a task that is causing an overallocation to another time (when the required resource is available) is to drag it to the required time (see Moving Linked Tasks on page 81 for an example). When moving a linked task you may receive Planning Wizard warnings (also covered on page 81) which necessitate removing links. So following this rescheduling you should relink the moved task in an appropriate way.

In a similar way we can split a task and move the split parts to times when the required resource is available (see Splitting Tasks on page 80).

Reallocating Tasks
To reallocate a task, select the task, click the Assign Resources button to open the dialog box, click the Replace button and select the new resource when prompted.

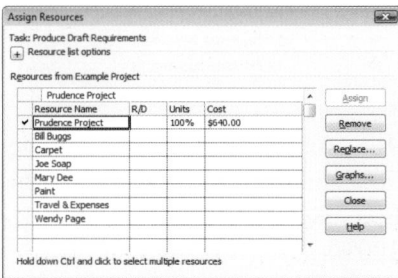

Overtime Working

In addition to allocating more resources, rescheduling or reallocating a task, we can leave a task allocated where it is but complete it sooner by scheduling overtime working.

In the following example, let us say that we need to have task 4.1 (Design Work) completed as early as possible and the resource assigned to it has agreed to work 2 additional hours (overtime) per day on this task.

	ⓘ	Task Name	Duration	Start	Sep 17, '07 S M T W T F S	Sep 24, '07 S M T W T F S
27		− 4 Design & Build Stage	20 days	Mon 9/17/07		
28		4.1 Design Work	5 days	Mon 9/17/07		Prudence Proj
29		4.2 Build Work	10 days	Mon 9/24/07		
30		4.3 Contingency	5 days	Mon 10/8/07		

1   Note the days that the task is being carried out

2   Select Tools>Change Working Time from the Menu bar and select the appropriate resource calendar

3   Enter a description on the Exception tab and the Start and Finish dates

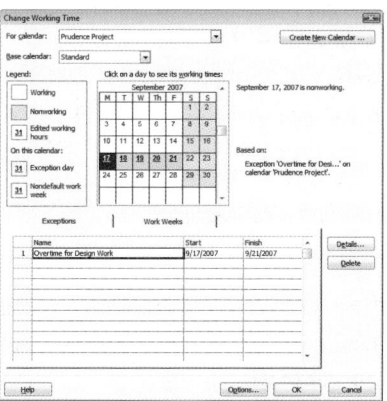

4   Click the Details button and enter the working time to include the 2 additional hours per day

	ⓘ	Task Name	Duration	Start	Sep 17, '07 S M T W T F S	Sep 24, '07 S M T W T F S
27		− 4 Design & Build Stage	19 days	Mon 9/17/07		
28		4.1 Design Work	5 days	Mon 9/17/07		Prudence Project
29		4.2 Build Work	10 days	Fri 9/21/07		
30		4.3 Contingency	5 days	Fri 10/5/07		

Note that the duration of the task remains 5 days but the work is completed in less time due to the 2 additional hours per day being worked by the allocated resource.

Task Constraints

When tasks are first entered into a project, they have the project start date as their start date (unless the project is backwards-scheduled, in which case they have the project finish date as their finish date). As they are linked and have resources assigned to them, they will be scheduled depending on their dependencies and resource availability and be given their own start and finish dates.

Sometimes these allocated start and finish dates are not viable in the real world and a start or finish date has to be imposed. When this happens in Project, it is called setting a task constraint.

Task constraints are set in the form of: must start or finish on a particular date; start no earlier or later than a particular date; finish no earlier or later than a particular date; start as soon as possible; or finish as late as possible. The default constraint which is applied to all tasks on a forward-scheduled project is: start as soon as possible. For a backward-scheduled project, the default constraint is start as late as possible.

Constraints can also be flexible or inflexible. A flexible constraint is one where the project finish date can be moved by the task. An inflexible constraint is one where the project finish date cannot be moved by the task. The following table lists the flexible constraint types and any limitations on that flexibility:

Constraint	Flexible for
As Soon As Possible	All projects
As Late As Possible	All projects
Finish No Earlier Than	Forward-scheduled projects
Start No Earlier Than	Forward-scheduled projects
Finish No Later Than	Backward-scheduled projects
Start No Later Than	Backward-scheduled projects

The *As Soon As Possible* and *As Late As Possible* constraints do not use a date, while all the others have a date associated with them. The date is the earliest or latest date that the task can or must start or finish (as appropriate to the type of constraint).

Applying Constraints

The usual reason for applying a constraint to a task is that some internal or external factor means that it can only happen at a certain time. As an example, a good time to start using a new financial system is often the start of a new financial year. So in this case you might want to set a "start no earlier" constraint.

1 In Gantt chart view select the task you wish to apply the constraint to and double-click on the Task Name to open the Task Information dialog box

	ⓘ	Task Name	Duration	Start	Oct 15, '07	Oct 22, '07	Oct 29, '07
					F S S M T W T F	S S M T W T F S	S M T W T F S
31		− 5 Implementation Stage	40 days	Fri 10/12/07			
32		5.1 Train Users	5 days	Fri 10/12/07			
33		5.2 Convert to New System	5 days	Fri 10/19/07			
34		5.3 Parallel Run	20 days	Fri 10/26/07			
35		5.4 Contingency	10 days	Fri 11/23/07			

2 Select the General tab and note the current start and finish dates for the task

3 Now select the Advanced tab, select the constraint type, set the constraint date, click OK and accept any warnings

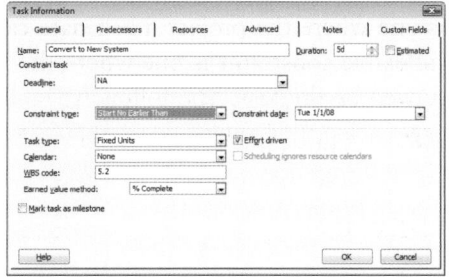

The constraint is set, the schedule is adjusted and a constraint symbol is added to the task information box.

	ⓘ	Task Name	Duration	Start	Oct '07	Nov '07	Dec '07	Jan '08	Feb '08
					1 8 15 22 29	5 12 19 26	3 10 17 24 31	7 14 21 28	4 11 18 25
31		− 5 Implementation Stage	91.5 days	Fri 10/12/07					
32		5.1 Train Users	5 days	Fri 10/12/07					
33		5.2 Convert to New System	5 days	Tue 1/1/08					
34		This task has a 'Start No Earlier Than' constraint on Tue 1/1/08.	20 days	Tue 1/8/08					
35			10 days	Tue 2/5/08					

As usual you can view the details of the constraint by positioning your pointer over the constraint symbol (as illustrated above). Note that as this has effectively introduced a two and a half month lag time between this task and the preceding task, the earlier tasks are no longer on the critical path.

137

Hot tip

In practice you would also want training to start as close as possible to the conversion date (a start "as late as possible" constraint would achieve this).

Constraint Conflicts

If you set a constraint that causes a conflict, the Planning Wizard appears, to warn you of the problem and offer suggestions for how you may be able to deal with it. As an example we will force a constraint conflict by setting a "must finish on" constraint on task 2.7.2 Present to Management (below).

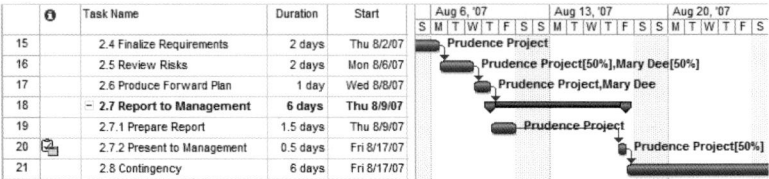

	❶	Task Name	Duration	Start
15		2.4 Finalize Requirements	2 days	Thu 8/2/07
16		2.5 Review Risks	2 days	Mon 8/6/07
17		2.6 Produce Forward Plan	1 day	Wed 8/8/07
18		− 2.7 Report to Management	6 days	Thu 8/9/07
19		2.7.1 Prepare Report	1.5 days	Thu 8/9/07
20		2.7.2 Present to Management	0.5 days	Fri 8/17/07
21		2.8 Contingency	6 days	Fri 8/17/07

1 Save your project before doing the following steps

2 Double-click on the relevant task to open the Task Information dialog box and check the current dates in the General tab

3 On the Advanced tab set a Must Finish On constraint, with the date of the preceding Friday. Click OK and the Planning Wizard will open giving you a warning and offering you three options

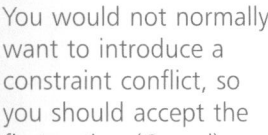

4 Select the third option (to force the constraint), click OK and accept any further warning and the task will be rescheduled

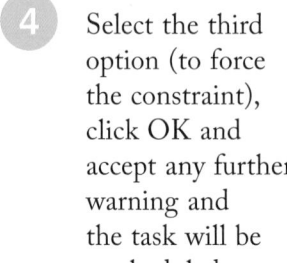
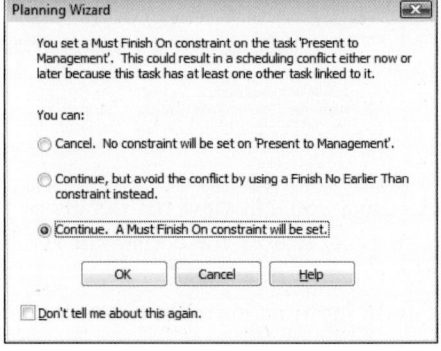

Viewing Constraints

When a task has a constraint applied to it, there will be a constraint symbol in the task information box. The constraint symbol looks like a small calendar and it will have a blue dot if it is a flexible constraint and a red dot if it is an inflexible constraint. If you pause your pointer over it a pop-up will display details of the constraint.

1 In Gantt chart view pause your pointer over a constraint symbol (the example on the right is the constraint set on the previous page)

	ⓘ	Task Name	Duration	Start
18		− 2.7 Report to Management	1.5 days	Thu 8/9/07
19		2.7.1 Prepare Report	1.5 days	Thu 8/9/07
20		2.7.2 Present to Management	0.5 days	Fri 8/10/07
21		This task has a 'Must Finish On' constraint on Fri 8/10/07.	6 days	Mon 8/13/07
22		The calendar 'Management Meetings' is assigned to the task.	5 days	Tue 8/21/07
23			5 days	Tue 8/21/07
24		3.2 Select Package	5 days	Tue 8/28/07

You can also view constraints by applying the Constraints Dates table to the Gantt chart view.

2 Select View>Table>More Tables from the Menu bar to display the More Tables dialog box

3 Select Constraint Dates and click the Apply button to display the constraint details (as below)

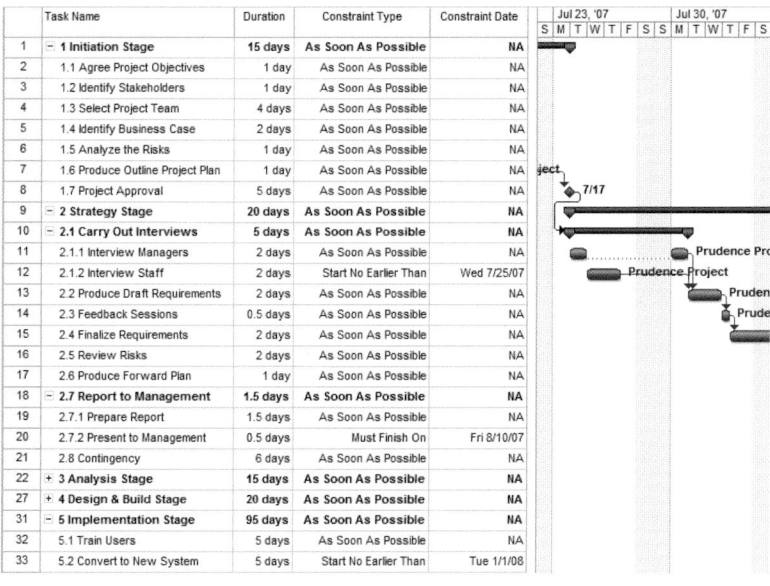

	Task Name	Duration	Constraint Type	Constraint Date
1	− 1 Initiation Stage	15 days	As Soon As Possible	NA
2	1.1 Agree Project Objectives	1 day	As Soon As Possible	NA
3	1.2 Identify Stakeholders	1 day	As Soon As Possible	NA
4	1.3 Select Project Team	4 days	As Soon As Possible	NA
5	1.4 Identify Business Case	2 days	As Soon As Possible	NA
6	1.5 Analyze the Risks	1 day	As Soon As Possible	NA
7	1.6 Produce Outline Project Plan	1 day	As Soon As Possible	NA
8	1.7 Project Approval	5 days	As Soon As Possible	NA
9	− 2 Strategy Stage	20 days	As Soon As Possible	NA
10	− 2.1 Carry Out Interviews	5 days	As Soon As Possible	NA
11	2.1.1 Interview Managers	2 days	As Soon As Possible	NA
12	2.1.2 Interview Staff	2 days	Start No Earlier Than	Wed 7/25/07
13	2.2 Produce Draft Requirements	2 days	As Soon As Possible	NA
14	2.3 Feedback Sessions	0.5 days	As Soon As Possible	NA
15	2.4 Finalize Requirements	2 days	As Soon As Possible	NA
16	2.5 Review Risks	2 days	As Soon As Possible	NA
17	2.6 Produce Forward Plan	1 day	As Soon As Possible	NA
18	− 2.7 Report to Management	1.5 days	As Soon As Possible	NA
19	2.7.1 Prepare Report	1.5 days	As Soon As Possible	NA
20	2.7.2 Present to Management	0.5 days	Must Finish On	Fri 8/10/07
21	2.8 Contingency	6 days	As Soon As Possible	NA
22	+ 3 Analysis Stage	15 days	As Soon As Possible	NA
27	+ 4 Design & Build Stage	20 days	As Soon As Possible	NA
31	− 5 Implementation Stage	95 days	As Soon As Possible	NA
32	5.1 Train Users	5 days	As Soon As Possible	NA
33	5.2 Convert to New System	5 days	Start No Earlier Than	Tue 1/1/08

Setting a Baseline

Once you have created your project plan, allocated resources, resolved any conflicts and are happy with the project schedule, you are ready to set a baseline.

A baseline represents a record of a set point in time where you have agreed and fixed your project plan. Project can hold up to eleven baselines for each project, named Baseline (for the first one) and then Baseline 1 to Baseline 10.

The first baseline you set should contain the original plan only; subsequent baselines will contain the current plan with any actual data up to that point.

When you set a baseline the dates, times and other data are recorded for all tasks.

Hot tip

Baselines 1 to 10 can also be selected in the Save Baseline dialog box and previously saved baselines can be updated by saving them again.

1. In Gantt chart view, select Tools>Tracking>Set Baseline from the Menu bar to open the Set Baseline dialog box

2. Select Set baseline and For: Entire project and click OK to save the baseline

3. Select Project>Project Information from the Menu bar to open the Project Information dialog box, and click the Statistics button to view the current, baseline and actual details for the project

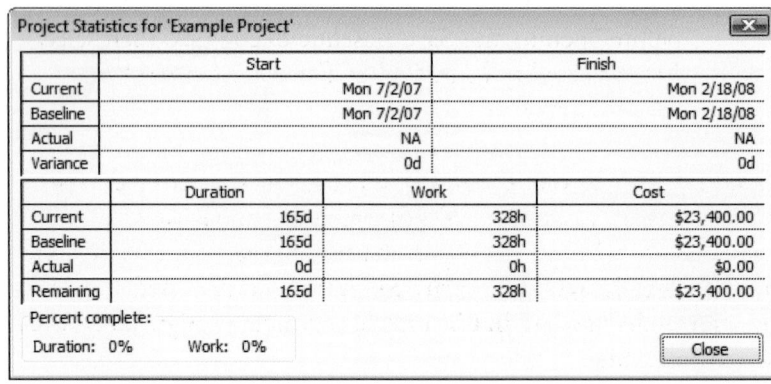

Project Statistics for 'Example Project'				
	Start		**Finish**	
Current		Mon 7/2/07		Mon 2/18/08
Baseline		Mon 7/2/07		Mon 2/18/08
Actual		NA		NA
Variance		0d		0d
	Duration	**Work**		**Cost**
Current	165d	328h		$23,400.00
Baseline	165d	328h		$23,400.00
Actual	0d	0h		$0.00
Remaining	165d	328h		$23,400.00

Percent complete:

Duration: 0%   Work: 0%

Interim Plans

As well as setting up to 11 baselines (which should be retained throughout the project) you can also create up to ten interim plans during the course of the project.

You may wish to create a new baseline at the end of each project stage to reflect any changes to the project that have been agreed during that stage. But you may also wish to use interim plans to track more detailed changes to the project.

While a baseline saves a lot of information about a project, an interim plan just saves details of the current task start and end dates.

1   In Gantt chart view, select Tools>Tracking>Set Baseline from the Menu bar to open the Set Baseline dialog box

2   Select Set interim plan, select Copy: Start/Finish, select Into: Start 1/Finish 1, select For: Entire project and click OK

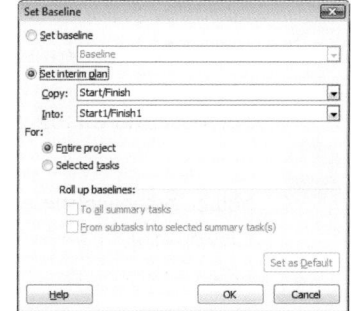

3   As the project progresses you can copy into Start 2/Finish 2 and so on

4   You can also update any existing interim plans by copying new information over the information previously saved

5   If you want to save interim plans for just the current stage of the project, select the tasks in the Gantt chart before opening the Save Baseline dialog box, then select For: Selected tasks instead of For: Entire project in Step 2 (above)

Interim plans are very useful for tracking changes made during a project stage. Then at the end stage review you will be able to look back and see what was changed and when. They can also be used for tracking changes during the whole project, and used as part of the end project review, but in practice baselines are probably more suitable for this.

Clearing a Baseline

Beware

Clearing a baseline is not possible in versions before Project 2002.

As well as updating baselines and interim plans, you can also clear them for the whole project, or for selected tasks.

1 Select Tools>Tracking>Clear Baseline from the Menu bar to open the Clear Baseline dialog box

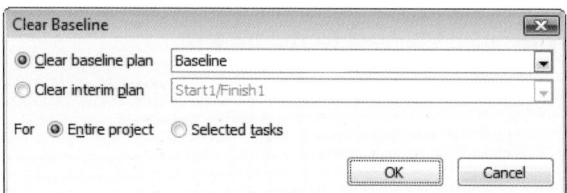

2 Select Clear baseline plan, select For: Entire project and click OK to clear the baseline

3 Select Project>Project Information and click the Statistics button to confirm that the baseline data has gone

4 To clear selected tasks, first select the task names in Gantt chart view

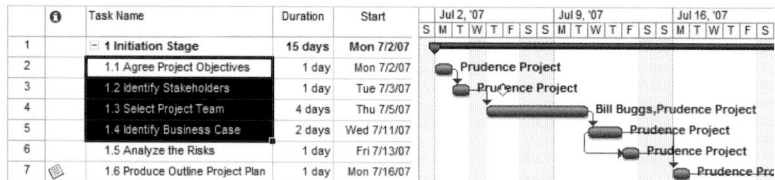

5 Select Tools>Tracking>Clear Baseline from the Menu bar to reopen the Clear Baseline dialog box

6 Select Clear interim plan, select Start 1/Finish 1, select Selected tasks and click OK

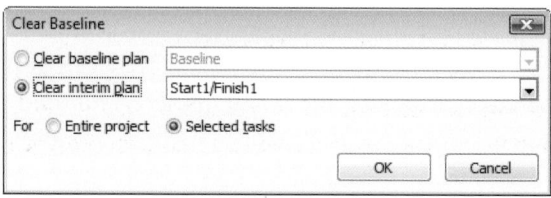

Stage Reviews

The project stages represent the strategic (top-level) view of the project. While project managers need to get down into the detailed work during a stage, they also need to keep a focus at the strategic-level (the big picture). This is the level that the project sponsor operates on, so the stage boundaries are the point where they share this strategic focus.

Milestones

The stage boundaries represent major milestones in a project and they offer the chance for the project to be reviewed strategically, before the next stage of the project starts. They can provide formal checkpoints, which will allow an out of control project to be stopped.

Review of Progress

Stage reviews provide a chance to look back at how the project has worked out so far. A chance to identify what has worked well and where there have been problems. An opportunity to learn from experience and compare the actual results (time, cost and deliverables) with the plan.

One common cause of projects going wrong is uncontrolled change (scope creep). Stage reviews are a good time to review the number of changes and the impact they have had.

Forward Plan

Based on what has happened so far, we can now revise the project plan as necessary to reflect what we have learned. Having done this we can re-examine the risks and finally review the business case to see if it still adds up.

End Stage Report

The results of the review and the forward plan can then be used to put together the End Stage Report, containing all of the above together with the project manager's comments and recommendations.

Stage Reviews

The stage review (formal or informal) should then take place between the project manager and project sponsor. The discussions and any decisions taken should be recorded, by the project manager, along with the formal decision to proceed (or not) with the project.

Hot tip

Stage reviews (formal or informal) give you the chance to step back from the detail and look at the big picture, with your project sponsor.

Summary

- Resource conflicts occur when the scheduled work cannot be carried out by the assigned resources in the required time frame

- The resource management toolbar provides some useful aids in investigating resource conflicts

- Project offers two options for resource leveling: manual (where you tell it when to level) and automatic (where leveling is performed continually)

- Project may have difficulty with leveling if you have used resource profiling (varying percentage availability)

- Manual adjustments can be made by allocating more resources to a task, rescheduling or splitting a task, reallocating tasks to a different resource, or overtime working

- Task constraints can be applied manually or through the leveling process and they determine when a task can or must start or finish

- Constraints can be applied on the advanced tab of the task information dialog box, or by setting the start or end date of a task

- Project will flag a constraint conflict if a constraint you are trying to apply can or will have an impact on another task

- Tasks with a constraint will have a constraint symbol in their task information box or details of all constraints can be displayed by applying the constraints dates table

- Baselines (up to 11) can be set for the whole project or selected tasks and can be used in progress reporting

- Interim plans (up to 10) can be set for the whole project or selected tasks, e.g. for a project stage

- Baselines and interim plans can be updated (replaced) or cleared

- Stage reviews are the ideal opportunity to review project progress against plan, with your project sponsor

12 Viewing Data

Project holds a vast amount of information on your project and provides many options for selecting and viewing it. This chapter covers the different ways of viewing, grouping, filtering, sorting and displaying the information.

Views

In Project, views are the way that data is displayed for you to look at and work on. They can be placed into two main categories: task views and resource views. There are 18 task views and 6 resource views. You normally use task views when working with task information and resource views when working with resource information. The views can be further divided into sheets, charts, graphs and forms.

Sheets

Sheets (similar to spreadsheets) display information in rows and columns with each task or resource being a row (horizontal) and each field in the task or resource being a column (vertical).

Charts and Graphs

Charts display graphical information in chart form, typical examples being the Gantt Chart and Network Diagram views. Graphs are used to display statistical information graphically in views, such as Resource Graph and Calendar.

Forms

Forms are used for the display and entry of detailed information on a task or resource.

Some views (such as Calendar) are simple, single views and some are compound views (such as Gantt Chart which shows a sheet on the left and a chart on the right). You can also display a single view or two views (one above the other). The example below is a compound view with the Gantt Chart (table and chart) in the upper half and the Task Form in the lower half.

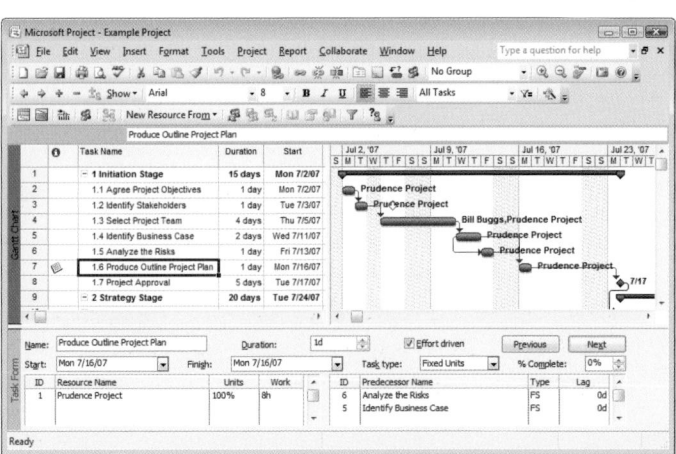

Tables

When working in a sheet view there are a number of preset tables that can be used (applied) to access different types of information on tasks or resources. There are 17 task tables that can be applied to task views and 10 resource tables applicable to resource views.

If the view you have currently selected is not displaying quite the right information, you can apply a different table to change the view. The tasks or resources displayed remain the same but you will see different bits of information for them.

1 In Gantt chart view select View>Table: Cost from the Menu bar, to replace the Task: Entry table

	Task Name	Fixed Cost	Fixed Cost Accrual	Total Cost	Jul 2, '07 S M T W T F S	Jul 9, '07 S M T W T F S
1	– 1 Initiation Stage	$0.00	Prorated	$3,360.00		
2	1.1 Agree Project Objectives	$0.00	Prorated	$320.00	Prudence Project	
3	1.2 Identify Stakeholders	$0.00	Prorated	$320.00	Prudence Project	
4	1.3 Select Project Team	$0.00	Prorated	$1,440.00		Bill Buggs,
5	1.4 Identify Business Case	$0.00	Prorated	$640.00		Prud
6	1.5 Analyze the Risks	$0.00	Prorated	$320.00		Pr
7	1.6 Produce Outline Project Plan	$0.00	Prorated	$320.00		
8	1.7 Project Approval	$0.00	Prorated	$0.00		

Hot tip

There are several more cost fields in the table, which can be seen by moving the vertical divider (shown in black).

147

2 Select View>Task Usage from the Menu bar to open Task Usage view

3 Then select View>Table: to change the table from Usage view to show the work details

Task Name	Work	Baseline	Variance	Actual	Details	Jul 2, '07 M	T	W	T	F
– Initiation Stage	80 hrs	80 hrs	0 hrs	0 hrs	Work	8h	8h		9.2h	11.6h
– Agree Project Objectives	8 hrs	8 hrs	0 hrs	0 hrs	Work	8h				
Prudence Project	8 hrs	8 hrs	0 hrs	0 hrs	Work	8h				
– Identify Stakeholders	8 hrs	8 hrs	0 hrs	0 hrs	Work		8h			
Prudence Project	8 hrs	8 hrs	0 hrs	0 hrs	Work		8h			
– Select Project Team	32 hrs	32 hrs	0 hrs	0 hrs	Work				9.2h	11.6h
Prudence Project	16 hrs	16 hrs	0 hrs	0 hrs	Work				1.2h	3.6h
Bill Buggs	16 hrs	16 hrs	0 hrs	0 hrs	Work				8h	8h

4 Try applying the various different tables to the views that you use to see what is available

5 When you have finished you can apply the default views back (Table: Entry for the Gantt chart view and Table: Usage for the Task Usage view)

Grouping

Grouping allows you to view your project tasks or resources grouped by any defined criteria. This can be applied to most task and resource views but not Calendar, Network Diagram, Relationship Diagram, Resource Graph and Form views. Each view has various standard groups to select from.

1 In Resource Sheet view, click the down arrow to the right of the Group By field to get the drop-down list

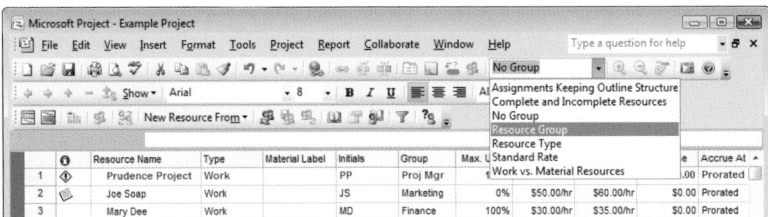

2 Select Resource Group in the drop-down list and the resource sheet is rearranged by resource within group, as in the following illustration

3 Try selecting the various other Group By options in the drop-down list

4 To return to the standard view just select No Groups in the Group By options

5 Now select View>Gantt Chart, select Show>Outline Level 1, then select Group By>Constraint Type (see the example at the top of the next page)

In the following illustration, the summary tasks are no longer displayed and, in their place, the tasks are now grouped under the constraint types.

❶	Task Name	Duration	Start	Finish	Jul 23, '07 M T W T F S S	Jul 30, '07 M T W T F S
	⊞ Constraint Type: As Soon As Possible	165 days	Mon 7/2/07	Mon 2/18/08		
	⊟ Constraint Type: Must Finish On	1 day	Fri 8/10/07	Fri 8/10/07		
📅📅	2.7.2 Present to Management	0.5 days	Fri 8/10/07	Fri 8/10/07		
	⊟ Constraint Type: Start No Earlier Than	119 days	Wed 7/25/07	Mon 1/7/08	▽	
📅	2.1.2 Interview Staff	2 days	Wed 7/25/07	Thu 7/26/07	▬ Prudence Project	
📅	5.2 Convert to New System	5 days	Tue 1/1/08	Mon 1/7/08		

This is a useful view to see which constraints you have set on which tasks. The Summary Tasks group behaves in the same way as the normal summary tasks and the view can be expanded and contracted by clicking the small plus or minus sign beside the group name.

The other useful feature is that Project rolls up totals by these groupings for you, useful for monitoring costs and work effort.

6 In Gantt chart view select Group By>Critical to apply this new grouping to the Gantt chart view

7 Now select View>Table: Work from the Menu bar to display the rolled-up work effort totals on the critical and non-critical summary lines

Task Name	Work	Baseline	Variance	Jul 2, '07 S M T W T F S	Jul 9, '07 S M T W T F S	Jul 16, '07 S M T W T F S	Jul 23, '07 S M T W T F S
⊟ Critical: No	176 hrs	176 hrs	0 hrs				
2.1.2 Interview Staff	16 hrs	16 hrs	0 hrs				▬ Prud
2.8 Contingency	0 hrs	0 hrs	0 hrs				
3.1 Agree Requirements	40 hrs	40 hrs	0 hrs				
3.2 Select Package	40 hrs	40 hrs	0 hrs				
3.3 Purchase Package	16 hrs	16 hrs	0 hrs				
3.4 Contingency	24 hrs	24 hrs	0 hrs				
4.1 Design Work	40 hrs	40 hrs	0 hrs				
4.2 Build Work	0 hrs	0 hrs	0 hrs				
4.3 Contingency	0 hrs	0 hrs	0 hrs				
5.1 Train Users	0 hrs	0 hrs	0 hrs				
⊟ Critical: Yes	182 hrs	182 hrs	0 hrs				
1.1 Agree Project Objectives	8 hrs	8 hrs	0 hrs	▬ Prudence Project			
1.2 Identify Stakeholders	8 hrs	8 hrs	0 hrs	▬ Prudence Project			
1.3 Select Project Team	32 hrs	32 hrs	0 hrs	▬ Bill Buggs,Prudence Project			
1.4 Identify Business Case	16 hrs	16 hrs	0 hrs	▬ Prudence Project			
1.5 Analyze the Risks	8 hrs	8 hrs	0 hrs	▬ Prudence Project			
1.6 Produce Outline Project Plan	8 hrs	8 hrs	0 hrs	▬ Prudence Project			

8 Now try out the other Group By options on the Gantt chart and also take a look at the group by options on the other views

Hot tip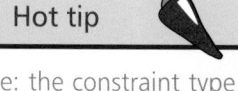

Note: the constraint type As Soon As Possible has been closed up in this illustration as this is the default and not really a constraint.

Customized Groups

While there are a good number of standard Group By options built into the standard views, you may also wish to define your own custom groups. You can define these based on one or more criteria and the color, pattern and font of the group bands can also be customized along with the sequence of sorting:

1 In Gantt chart view select Project>Group By>Customize Group By from the Menu bar to open the Customize Group By dialog box

2 In Group By Field Name, select the required field from the drop down list (Resource Names in our example)

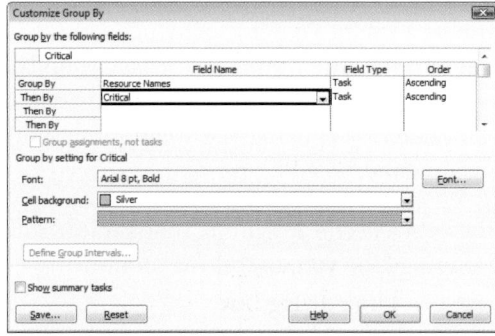

3 In Then By Field Name select your second required field from the drop down list (Critical in the example above)

4 Continue selecting any further Group By fields as required, then click OK to create the custom group

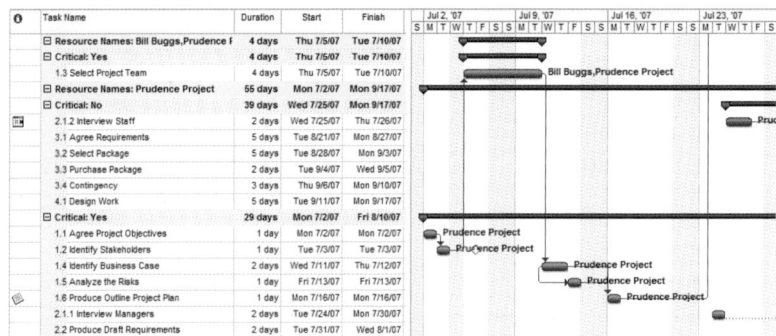

The example shows tasks grouped by resource and critical. Font, size and style and cell background and pattern can also be set in the Customize Group By dialog box.

Fiscal Year

Project allows you to set the use of the fiscal year for the top, middle or bottom tier timescales. The following example shows how this can be used where the fiscal (business) year is different from the calendar year.

Beware

The third tier timescale is not available in versions before Project 2002.

1 In Gantt chart view select Tools>Change Working Time>Options from the Menu bar to open the Calendar Options dialog box

2 Change Fiscal year starts in: to April, select Use starting year for FY numbering and click OK. Click OK again to close Working Time dialog box

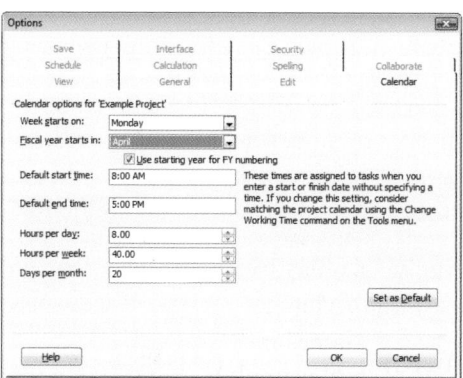

3 Select Format>Timescale from the Menu bar to open the Timescale dialog box

4 On the Middle Tier set Units to Years and deselect Use fiscal year. On the Bottom Tier set Units to Quarters, Use fiscal year and click OK.

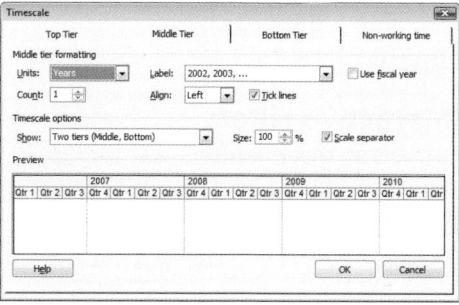

The major timescale now displays calendar years and the minor scale displays fiscal quarters (as below)

	ⓘ	Task Name	Duration	Start	Finish	2007				2008			
						Qtr 4	Qtr 1	Qtr 2	Qtr 3	Qtr 4	Qtr 1	Qtr 2	Qtr 3
1		+ 1 Initiation Stage	15 days	Mon 7/2/07	Mon 7/23/07		▼▼						
9		+ 2 Strategy Stage	20 days	Tue 7/24/07	Mon 8/20/07		▼▼						
22		+ 3 Analysis Stage	15 days	Tue 8/21/07	Mon 9/10/07			▼▼					
27		+ 4 Design & Build Stage	20 days	Tue 9/11/07	Mon 10/8/07			▼▼					
31		+ 5 Implementation Stage	95 days	Mon 10/8/07	Mon 2/18/08				▼━━━▼				

Filters

In addition to its other selection capabilities, Project also allows you to filter and sort data before viewing (or printing). Filtering allows you to select just the information that you wish to be displayed.

Predefined Filters

There are a number of predefined filters that you can use to select things, such as late tasks, tasks in progress, work that is over budget, and so on. Project contains 32 predefined task filters and 23 predefined resource filters. In addition to these, you can also create your own custom filters to meet any specific requirements.

Filters can be used to focus on certain tasks in your project or on specific resources in the project. When you apply a filter, only the tasks or resources that meet the filter criteria are displayed. All other tasks and resources are hidden while you are using a filter.

Applying filters to your project does not change the data in any way, it just changes the way it is displayed.

AutoFilter

Project contains an AutoFilter feature which gives you a quick way of finding particular information in a field. When it's turned on, each column heading has an arrow on the right-hand side which can be used to apply a filter to the information in that column. You can apply filters to as many columns as you like and, once a filter has been applied to a column, the column title turns blue.

Interactive Filters

As well as specific filters you can apply interactive filters which display a dialog box during the filtering process. You then provide the information to the dialog box to allow Project to complete the filtering process.

Custom Filters

If none of the predefined filters meet your requirements you can create a custom filter that exactly matches your needs. You can copy an existing filter and then edit it to meet your needs or you can create a completely new filter. The Filter Definition dialog box provides shortcuts to simplify this process.

Examples of all these filters are given in the next few topics.

AutoFilter

When AutoFilter is turned on, you can apply filters to any column. The All filter will remove any filter criteria and the Custom filter allows a column to be filtered by more than one criterion. The following example will demonstrate filtering on task duration.

1 Select View>More Views>Task Sheet from the Menu bar, click Apply and then View all subtasks

2 Select View>Table>Usage from the Menu bar to apply the usage table

3 Click the AutoFilter button on the toolbar and the filter down arrows will appear on the column headings

Task Name ▼	Work ▼	Duration ▼	Start ▼	Finish ▼
− **Initiation Stage**	**80 hrs**	**15 days**	**Mon 7/2/07**	**Mon 7/23/07**
Agree Project Objectives	8 hrs	1 day	Mon 7/2/07	Mon 7/2/07
Identify Stakeholders	8 hrs	1 day	Tue 7/3/07	Tue 7/3/07
Select Project Team	32 hrs	4 days	Thu 7/5/07	Tue 7/10/07
Identify Business Case	16 hrs	2 days	Wed 7/11/07	Thu 7/12/07
Analyze the Risks	8 hrs	1 day	Fri 7/13/07	Fri 7/13/07
Produce Outline Project Plan	8 hrs	1 day	Mon 7/16/07	Mon 7/16/07
Project Approval	0 hrs	5 days	Tue 7/17/07	Mon 7/23/07

4 Click the Duration down arrow and select >1 day (greater than 1 day) to only display tasks of over 1 day duration (note the Duration column heading turns blue)

5 Change the Duration filter back to All then click the Work down arrow and select Custom

6 Select the required filter or filters and click OK to apply the filter

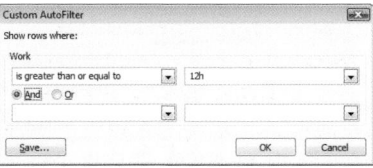

7 Click AutoFilter again to turn it off

153

Hot tip

You can save any AutoFilter setting as a Custom filter for future use by clicking the Save button.

Filter Criteria

You can specify filter criteria interactively if you often need to make similar enquiries but with slightly different parameters. This is preferable to creating a large number of custom filters.

For example, you might want to get details of all tasks that are scheduled during the summer, to check for any vacation implications.

1 Select View>More Views>Task Sheet from the Menu bar and click Apply, then select View>Table>Schedule

2 Select Project>Filtered For>Date Range from the Menu bar to open the Date Range dialog box

3 Enter or select the From date and click OK

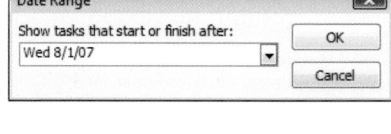

4 Enter or select the To date and click OK to display only the tasks in the selected range

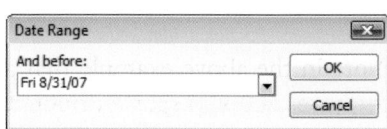

	Task Name	Start	Finish	Late Start	Late Finish
9	− Strategy Stage	Tue 7/24/07	Mon 8/20/07	Mon 7/23/07	Tue 11/6/07
13	Produce Draft Requirements	Tue 7/31/07	Wed 8/1/07	Mon 7/30/07	Tue 7/31/07
14	Feedback Sessions	Thu 8/2/07	Thu 8/2/07	Wed 8/1/07	Wed 8/1/07
15	Finalize Requirements	Thu 8/2/07	Mon 8/6/07	Wed 8/1/07	Fri 8/3/07
16	Review Risks	Mon 8/6/07	Wed 8/8/07	Fri 8/3/07	Tue 8/7/07
17	Produce Forward Plan	Wed 8/8/07	Thu 8/9/07	Tue 8/7/07	Wed 8/8/07
18	− Report to Management	Thu 8/9/07	Fri 8/10/07	Wed 8/8/07	Fri 8/10/07
19	Prepare Report	Thu 8/9/07	Fri 8/10/07	Wed 8/8/07	Thu 8/9/07
20	Present to Management	Fri 8/10/07	Fri 8/10/07	Fri 8/10/07	Fri 8/10/07
21	Contingency	Mon 8/13/07	Mon 8/20/07	Tue 10/30/07	Tue 11/6/07
22	− Analysis Stage	Tue 8/21/07	Mon 9/10/07	Wed 11/7/07	Tue 11/27/07
23	Agree Requirements	Tue 8/21/07	Mon 8/27/07	Wed 11/7/07	Tue 11/13/07
24	Select Package	Tue 8/28/07	Mon 9/3/07	Wed 11/14/07	Tue 11/20/07

In the example above we selected the whole of August. Any task that is in progress during August is displayed including tasks that start before August or end after August.

Select All Tasks on the filter down arrow to remove the filter.

Filter by Resource

You can use resource filters in a Task view to display all tasks assigned to a resource. In a Resource view you can use resource filters to select resources by Group.

1 Select View>Gantt Chart from the Menu bar

2 Click the Filter down arrow on the Toolbar and select Using Resource... (the three dots indicate further choices)

3 Click the down arrow, select the resource name and click OK

Note in the above example that all tasks assigned to the selected resource will be displayed (including tasks with additional resources assigned). The next example will filter by resource group in a resource view.

4 Select View>Resource Sheet from the Menu bar, click the Filter down arrow on the Toolbar and select Group...

5 Type in the name of the group and click OK to filter by the resource group

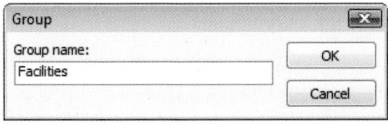

	ⓘ	Resource Name	Type	Material Label	Initials	Group	Max. Units	Std. Rate
6		Paint	Material	gallon		Facilities		$15.00
7		Carpet	Material	square yard		Facilities		$50.00

Note that there is no selection facility on the Group dialog box in Step 5 above, you have to type in the group name. Select All Resources from the Filter down arrow to remove the filter.

Custom Filters

Custom filters can be created from new or they can be created by editing an existing filter. A custom filter can have a single criterion or multiple criteria. For an example we will create a custom filter to only show tasks starting after September 01.

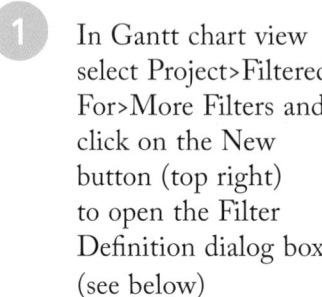

1 In Gantt chart view select Project>Filtered For>More Filters and click on the New button (top right) to open the Filter Definition dialog box (see below)

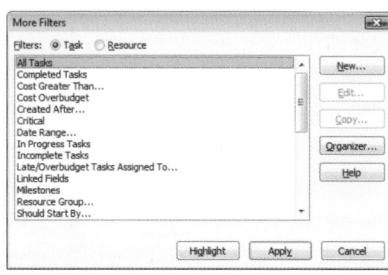

2 Type a name for the new filter and select Show in menu (top right)

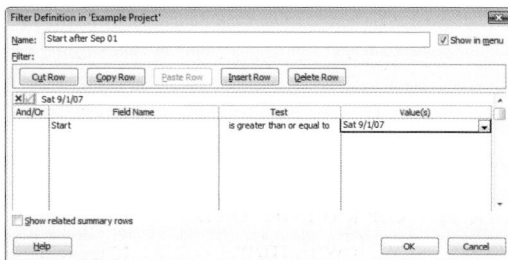

3 Click in the first Field Name and select Start, click in the Test column and select "is greater than or equal to" (as in the illustration above), then click in the Value column, select the required start date and click OK

5 The new filter is displayed in the More Filters dialog box, select it and click on the Apply button and the filter will be applied (as below)

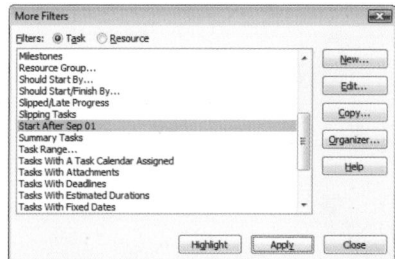

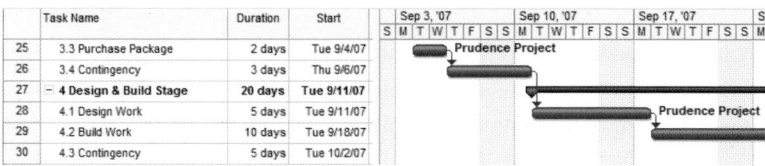

Sorting

Tasks and Resources are usually displayed in ascending ID Number sequence. However, you can sort the display by any field or a combination of fields by specifying sort keys.

The following example will identify the largest pieces of work by sorting the tasks by summary task and then tasks in descending duration sequence.

1 In Task Sheet view Show all subtasks and select View>Table>Usage from the Menu bar

2 Select Project>Sort>Sort By from the Menu bar to open the Sort dialog box

3 Click on the Sort by down arrow, select Summary and select Descending

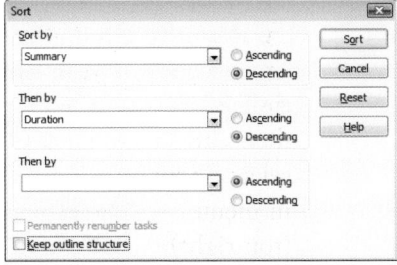

4 Click on the Then by down arrow, select Duration and Descending

5 Uncheck Keep outline structure and click the Sort button to sort the tasks into the desired sequence (as illustrated below)

	❶	Task Name	Work	Duration	Start	Finish
31		⊟ Implementation Stage	80 hrs	95 days	Mon 10/8/07	Mon 2/18/08
9		⊟ Strategy Stage	118 hrs	20 days	Tue 7/24/07	Mon 8/20/07
27		⊟ Design & Build Stage	40 hrs	20 days	Tue 9/11/07	Mon 10/8/07
1		⊟ Initiation Stage	80 hrs	15 days	Mon 7/2/07	Mon 7/23/07
22		⊟ Analysis Stage	120 hrs	15 days	Tue 8/21/07	Mon 9/10/07
10		⊟ Carry Out Interviews	32 hrs	5 days	Tue 7/24/07	Mon 7/30/07
18		⊟ Report to Management	14 hrs	1.5 days	Thu 8/9/07	Fri 8/10/07
34		Parallel Run	0 hrs	20 days	Tue 1/8/08	Mon 2/4/08
29		Build Work	0 hrs	10 days	Tue 9/18/07	Mon 10/1/07
35		Contingency	0 hrs	10 days	Tue 2/5/08	Mon 2/18/08
21		Contingency	0 hrs	6 days	Mon 8/13/07	Mon 8/20/07
8		Project Approval	0 hrs	5 days	Tue 7/17/07	Mon 7/23/07
23		Agree Requirements	40 hrs	5 days	Tue 8/21/07	Mon 8/27/07
24		Select Package	40 hrs	5 days	Tue 8/28/07	Mon 9/3/07
28		Design Work	40 hrs	5 days	Tue 9/11/07	Mon 9/17/07

Hot tip

Combining sorting with filters gives you a powerful range of features for viewing your data.

Highlight Filters

When Tasks and Resources are filtered, those that do not meet the filter criteria are hidden from view. Highlight filters can be used so that all tasks or resources remain visible, but the tasks or resources that meet the filter criteria are highlighted in blue.

1 In Gantt Chart view, Show all subtasks and select Project>Filter For>More Filters from the Menu bar to open the More Filters dialog box

2 Select the required filter criteria (Resource Group in this example) and click Highlight

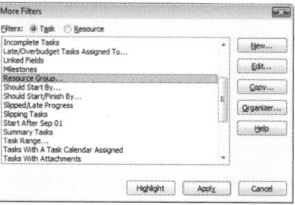

3 The Resource Group dialog box will open, type in the name of the resource group to be filtered and click OK

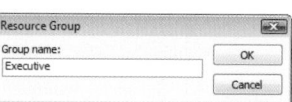

The resources belonging to the selected resource group will be highlighted in blue, as in the following example.

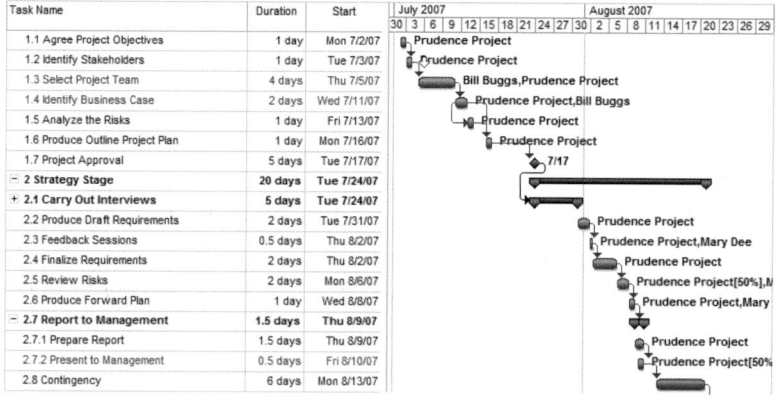

4 Click the Filter down arrow on the Toolbar and select All Tasks to return the display to normal again

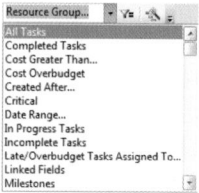

Background Highlighting

With the introduction of Background Cell Highlighting in Project 2007, you can now change the background color of cells or rows to convey additional meaning to the data.

For example we may wish to highlight certain problem tasks in a report to management.

1 In Gantt Chart view select the task you wish to highlight by clicking in the Task ID (to select the whole task) and select Format>Font from the Menu bar to open the Font dialog box

2 Select the down arrow beside Background Color: and select the desired color from the drop-down list

3 Click OK to apply the background

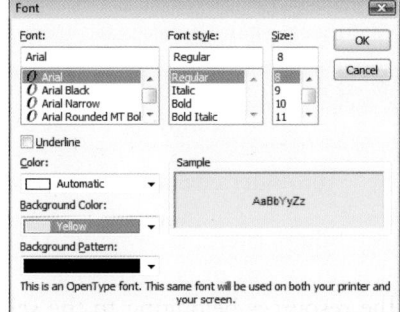

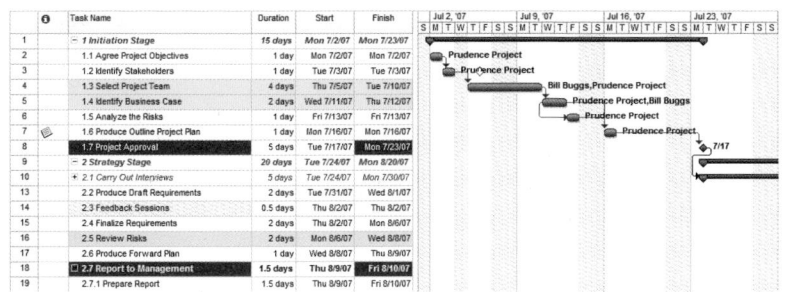

As well as applying background highlighting, the Font dialog box allows you to edit the font, font style, size and color. The background highlighting also allows you to change the background pattern. This gives significant scope for highlighting.

Summary

- Views are the ways that Project displays data on the screen. They consist of sheets (like spreadsheets), charts and graphs (visual) and forms (for detailed data entry)

- When working in a sheet view there are a number of different tables that can be applied to vary the data in the sheet

- Grouping allows you to group the data by resource and various other options

- In addition to the standard groups, you can create your own customized groups by selecting the required fields

- Fiscal year allows you to work with a non-calendar year

- Filters enable you to select which tasks or resources are displayed according to selection criteria

- AutoFilter enables you to select a filter on one or more columns

- Filter criteria allow you to specify more complex filters based on ranges or comparisons

- Tasks and resources can be filtered by resource or resource group

- Custom filters can be defined either as new filters or based on an existing filter. These can be compound filters with several criteria

- In addition to filtering, sorting allows the sequence in which tasks or other data are displayed to be defined using up to three parameters

- Highlight filters allow all data to remain visible but with the data that meets the filter criteria being highlighted in blue

- Background cell highlighting allows cells or rows to be highlighted in various colors independent of the data, for information purposes

- In addition to the background highlighting, the fonts can also be varied as required

13 Printing Reports

This chapter covers the setup, preview and printing of charts and reports. It deals with headers and footers and the useful copy picture function.

Printing a View

Any chart or table view can be printed using the print button on the Toolbar. However it is worthwhile setting the view up correctly before you print it.

1 To print a Gantt chart view, first format the screen to show the information you want to appear on the print by showing the appropriate level of subtasks

2 Then move the vertical divider to cover or expose any fields on the table (left-hand panel)

3 Zoom in or out to get the view you want on the Gantt chart (right-hand panel)

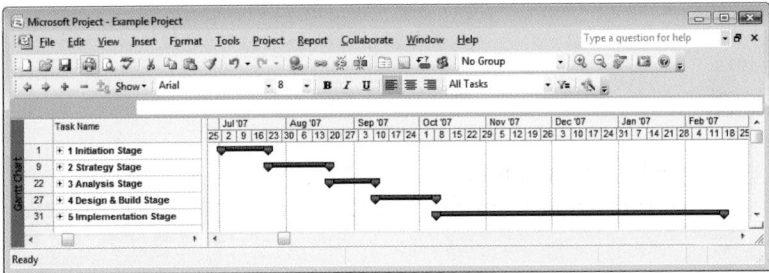

4 Click on the Print button on the Toolbar to print the view

5 To print a Resource sheet view, format the screen to show the information you wish to print by adjusting the scrollbars and the right-hand side of the screen

6 To hide any columns in the middle of the screen right-click on the column header and select Hide column

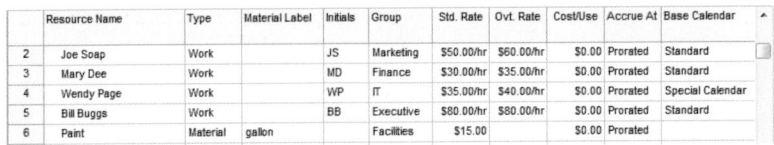

7 Click on the Print button on the Toolbar

Headers and Footers

In addition to the basic information displayed in a report, Project allows you to create your own headers (displayed at the top of each page) and footers (displayed at the bottom of each page). These are defined in the Page Setup dialog box.

You can enter any text you like and also include general system information, such as page number, date, project title, etc. You also have access to a wide range of project-level information.

1 Select File>Page Setup from the Menu bar to open the Page Setup dialog box

2 Select the Header tab at the top of the dialog box and the required Alignment tab in the center of the dialog box

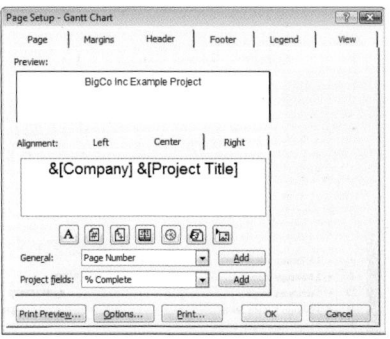

3 Select the required information from the General and Project field drop down lists (in the example we have selected Company Name and Project Title) and click the Add button

4 Select the Footer tab and add any required information (in the example we have added "of" and the Total Page Count)

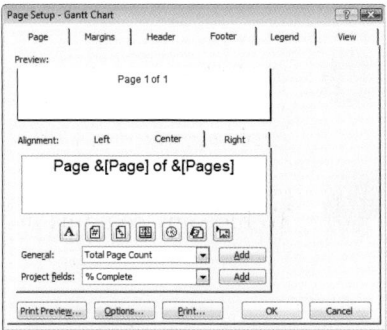

5 Click the OK button to save the header and footer information

6 Print your report or use print preview (see next topic)

Previewing Reports

With Project, it is always a good idea to preview a report before printing it. That way you can make sure it will look the way you want it to and make any final adjustments to it. It may also save you wasting a lot of paper.

1 Open your project file in Gantt chart view, Show all subtasks and zoom in to days within weeks view

2 Click the Print Preview button on the Toolbar (or select File>Print Preview from the Menu bar) to open the print preview screen

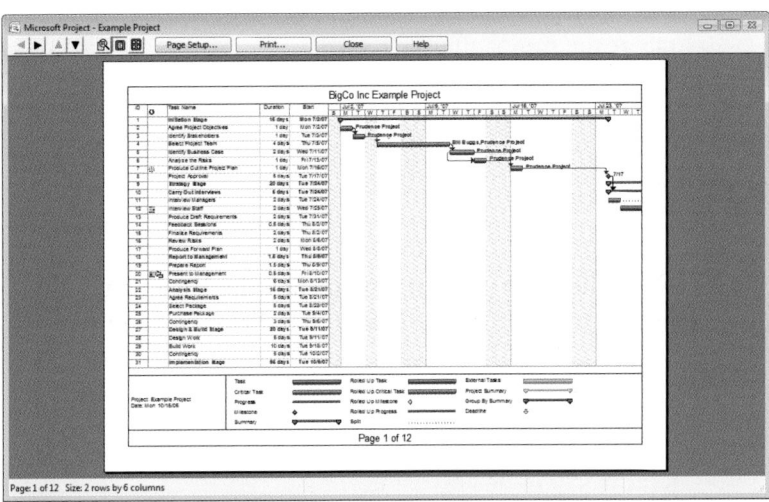

3 You can zoom the view in and out by clicking with your cursor (magnifying glass symbol) over the page

4 Click the Multiple Pages button (to the left of the Page Setup button) to show the complete printout

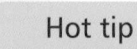
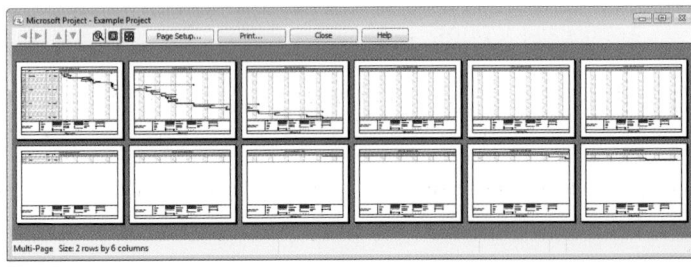

Page Setup and Scaling

In Project you can set the paper size and many other details from the Page Setup dialog box. You can also scale reports to get the best fit to a certain number of pages.

1   In Print Preview click the Page Setup button (or from normal view select File>Page Setup from the Menu bar) to open the Page Setup dialog box

2   Select the Page tab then scale by changing the Adjust to: percentage or select Fit to: and specify the number of pages wide and tall

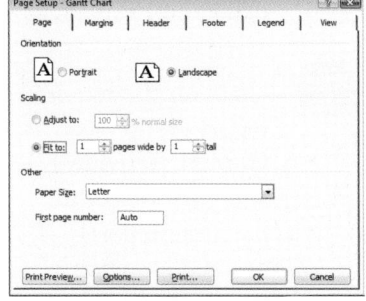

3   Click the Print Preview button to see how the print will look

4   From the print preview screen click the Page Setup button to return to the page setup dialog box to make further adjustments as necessary until you are satisfied with how your printout will look

5   Click OK to save the page setup information, then print your report

In the page setup dialog box you can also set the following:

- Select page orientation (portrait or landscape)

- Select paper size (letter, A4, etc.)

- Select starting page number

- Set margins and borders

- Specify legend information (lower part of the preview screen, see illustration opposite) and whether to repeat on each page

- Various other view options, such as information to repeat on all pages, printing notes, printing blank pages, etc.

Printing Reports

There are 22 predefined report formats, in 5 groups, available in Project. There is also a custom group, where you can create your own report formats, either based on an existing report format or starting from new.

1 Select Report>Reports from the Menu bar to open the Reports dialog box

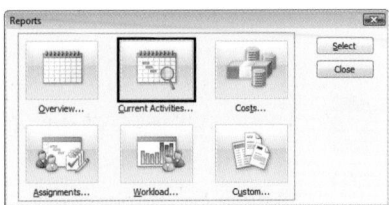

2 Click on the required report group (such as Current Activities) and click Select to open the reports group dialog box

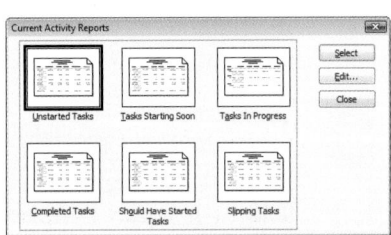

3 Click on the required report (such as Unstarted Tasks) and click Edit to open the Task Report dialog box

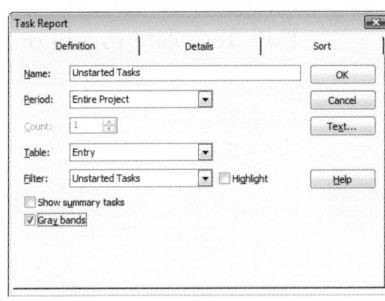

4 Change any information on the Definition, Details or Sort tabs

5 Click the Text button to edit the font details

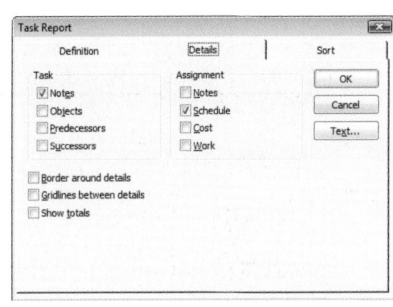

6 Click OK to return to the above reports group dialog box (as after Step 2)

7 Click Select to preview the report, then Print and OK to print it

Visual Reports

Visual reports allows you to view your project data in Pivot Table reports in Microsoft Office Excel or Pivot Diagram views in Microsoft Office Visio Professional. There are several Excel and Visio templates provided with Project. These can also be edited or you can create your own templates. As an example we will create a budget cost report from a template.

Beware

Visual Reports are a new feature in Project 2007 and are not available in earlier versions.

1 Select Report>Visual Reports from the Menu bar to open the Create Report dialog box

2 To limit the templates displayed check or uncheck the Excel and Visio check boxes at the top and select the category of report from the six category tabs

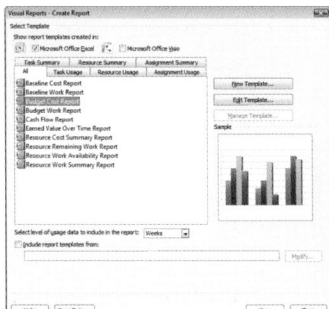

3 Select the report template you wish to use (e.g. Budget Cost Report), click Edit Template to add or remove any required fields, then click View to display the report in the target application (as below)

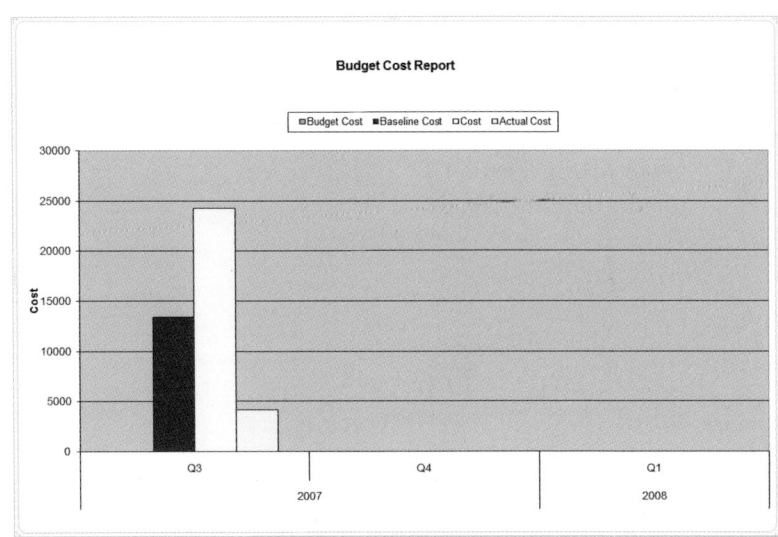

Copy Picture

The Copy Picture facility in Project is useful for including information, such as Gantt charts in project reports. It can be selected from the Report menu or using the Copy Picture button on the Toolbar.

1 First format your screen to show the information you require (in this example we are focusing on the work scheduled for the current month)

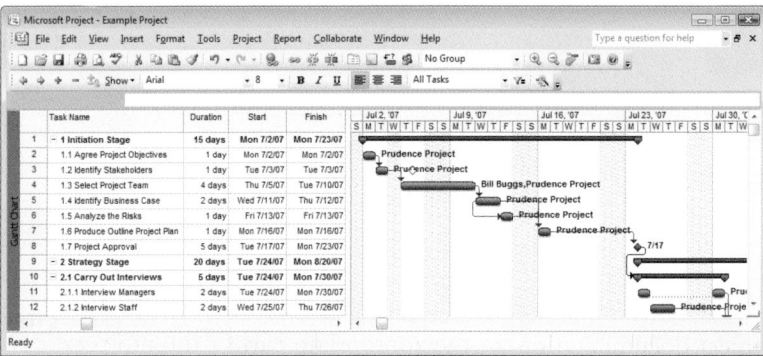

2 Click on the Copy Picture button on the Toolbar to open the Copy Picture dialog box

3 Select Render image for screen or printer as required, adjust the timescale if required and click OK

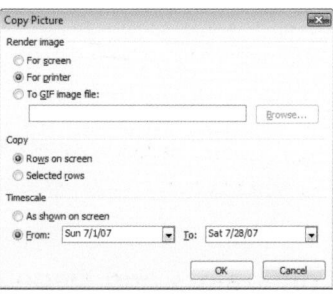

4 Open your target application (e.g. Word, PowerPoint, etc.) and paste the picture into the document in the required position using the Edit>Paste or Paste Special from the Menu bar in that application (as in the example right)

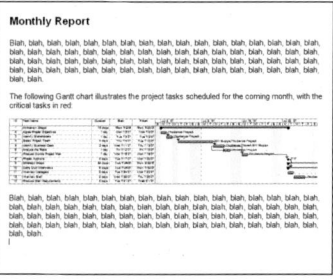

Progress Reports

Progress reports form one of the key control mechanisms in a project. They keep the project team informed, they keep the project sponsor informed and they can keep other project stakeholders informed (if applicable).

Frequency

The frequency of reporting on a project should be agreed between the project manager and project sponsor during project start up. Monthly is often the most appropriate reporting frequency, but whatever is agreed, it is important to have face to face reviews, backed up by written progress reports. These will form a permanent record as part of the project documentation. As a general rule, monthly reports should focus on stage and task completion (weekly reports would focus on task and subtask completion).

Format

The progress report itself should be word-processed (or in some other electronic form) so it can be retained as part of the formal project documentation, in the appropriate part of the project database or filing system. Whatever form it takes, it should be a simple, brief (ideally one-page) summary of progress. The following are some suggested main headings:

Achievements this Period

Stages, tasks and any key deliverables that were completed during the period since the previous report.

Problem Areas

Stages, tasks, or key deliverables that were scheduled to be completed during this period, but were not (with a brief reason). Any other problems or issues that have arisen in the project.

Constraints and Dependencies

Anything that could have an impact on the project (particularly if it is outside of the control of the project team) and anything the project is dependent on. This can help to warn the project sponsor of potential issues.

Project Plan Revisions

Any potential changes to a stage or the project completion date, functionality or cost. Any other revisions to the project needing to be formally agreed with the project sponsor.

Hot tip

A golden rule for progress reports is "no surprises". If there is bad news, tell your project sponsor in person.

Summary

- Any chart or table view can be printed using the print button on the toolbar, but it is worth spending a little time to format the printout first

- Headers and footers can be defined using the page setup dialog box and can include system and project information as well as any text information

- Before printing anything from Project, it is a very good idea to use print preview first. Then the format and layout can be checked (and changed if necessary) before printing. It can also help to prevent wasting paper as Project can sometimes generate quite a lot of empty or nearly empty pages

- Page setup can be used in Project in the normal way to control the format (orientation, paper size, margins and legends) of a report

- Scaling can be used to reduce the number of pages that will be printed or to ensure that all the required information appears together on the same page

- In addition to being able to print from any view, there are 22 predefined reports which can be printed and also customized to provide just the information you want to see

- Visual reports is a new feature that allows data to be passed in a seamless manner between Project and Microsoft Office Excel or Microsoft Office Visio Professional for manipulation and display

- Copy picture allows a snapshot of the screen to be taken (with some editing options) for pasting into a document in another application, such as Word or PowerPoint

- Progress reports form a key control mechanism in a project and in addition to any copied pictures, they should also list the project achievements together with any problems, constraints or plan revisions

14 Tracking Progress

Once the project is underway you need to update it with details of progress. This chapter covers the different types of progress information and how to deal with them.

Progress Tracking

Up to now, you have been planning your project, allocating resources to it and then scheduling when things will happen. Once the project is under way, though, you need to start tracking progress against your plan and schedule.

You enter information about progress by using actual start and completion dates as well as effort expended by resources.

If tasks are completed ahead of schedule, you can then decide if you want to bring other tasks forward. If tasks are running late, you can decide what actions you can take to help.

Again, the Gantt Chart is the most effective way of tracking progress as it can show actual against the plan.

Before you begin to enter actual information, complete your plan in as much detail as you are able, using contingency to allow for the unknown. Once you are happy with the plan you can set a baseline and then start progress tracking.

Project stores information under three headings:

Baseline
The plan dates which are stored when you set a baseline. These are used to compare with the actual and scheduled dates.

Actual
Actual work that has taken place on tasks, which have been completed or part completed.

Schedule
Tasks that have not yet been started or work still remaining to be done on part completed tasks.

The frequency with which you enter your information is up to you, but typically you would get progress details from the people working on the project at the end of each week.

As you enter your actual data the project is recalculated and rescheduled. So start at the earliest tasks on the schedule and work through. Once you have input all the actual information and seen the impact on the schedule you can re-evaluate the project and make any adjustments required to the project tasks to deal with issues that have arisen.

Progress Information

In addition to actual start and finish dates, you can also input progress information on the percentage completed, actual and remaining duration, actual and remaining work and actual and remaining cost. Depending on the type of information you input, Project will calculate the other relevant information.

If you input a task completion date, Project will set the actual start date to the scheduled start date and the actual duration to the difference between the start date and actual completion date.

The most accurate way of recording progress is to input the actual work done. This should be recorded by all the people resources you have working on the project. If this is less than the estimate for the task, Project will then calculate the work remaining as the difference between the actual work done and the original estimate.

As a minimum, you will need the following progress information from your project team at the end of each week:

- Tasks started

- Tasks and deliverables completed

- Hours worked on each task

- Estimated hours work to completion for each task

While Project's calculation of the work to completion may be acceptable at the beginning of a task, it is far more accurate to get people to record their own estimates of the work required to complete their tasks at the same time as they record the work done. You can then input this information and get a picture of the way the project is really going.

You can also input actual duration and, if that is less than the scheduled duration, Project calculates the remaining duration as the difference. If the task is actually completed in less than the scheduled duration, you need to set the remaining duration to zero. If it is going to be completed in less or more time you can again input your expected duration. In the same way, you can enter actual and remaining costs.

You can input this task progress information in a number of views including Gantt Chart, Task Usage and Resource Usage views.

Completed Work

Once a task has been completed, the easiest way to enter that information is simply by telling Project that the task is completed.

1 In Gantt chart view, click on the task name to select the completed task

2 Select Tools>Tracking>Update Tasks from the Menu bar to open the Update Tasks dialog box

3 Click the Actual Finish down arrow, select the actual finish date and click OK

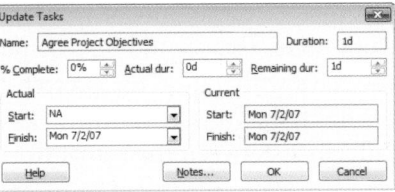

4 If you open the Update Tasks dialog box again you will note that the actual start has also been set, the task is 100% complete and the remaining duration is now zero

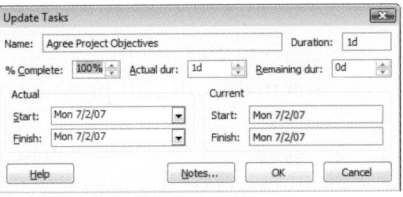

5 Note also that a progress line has been drawn through the task, the task bar has turned blue (it is no longer on the critical path as it has been completed) and a tick has been placed in the Task Information box

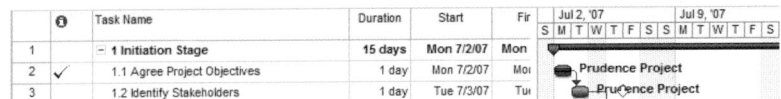

6 Position your cursor over the Task Information box to display the date completed

Part Completed Work

Where a number of days or hours of work have been carried out on a task, but the task is not yet fully completed, you can enter the actual work carried out.

1 In Task Usage view select Format>Details>Actual Work from the Menu bar to display details of Work (planned) and Actual Work (carried out)

	ⓘ	Task Name	Work	Duration	Start	Details	Jul 2, '07 M	T	W	T	F
1		− Initiation Stage	96 hrs	15 days	Mon 7/2	Work	8h	8h		9.2h	11.6h
						Act. W	8h				
2	✓	− Agree Project Objectives	8 hrs	1 day	Mon 7/2	Work	8h				
						Act. W	8h				
		Prudence Project	*8 hrs*		Mon 7/2	Work	8h				
						Act. W	8h				
3		− Identify Stakeholders	8 hrs	1 day	Tue 7/3	Work		8h			
						Act. W					
		Prudence Project	*8 hrs*		Tue 7/3	Work		8h			
						Act. W					
4		− Select Project Team	32 hrs	4 days	Thu 7/5	Work				9.2h	11.6h
						Act. W					

2 Click in the Actual Work field of the resource for which you wish to enter the details, type the number of hours of actual work and press Enter

	ⓘ	Task Name	Work	Duration	Start	Details	Jul 2, '07 M	T	W	T	F
1		− Initiation Stage	96 hrs	15 days	Mon 7/2	Work	8h	5h		12.2h	11.6h
						Act. W	8h	5h			
2	✓	− Agree Project Objectives	8 hrs	1 day	Mon 7/2	Work	8h				
						Act. W	8h				
		Prudence Project	*8 hrs*		Mon 7/2	Work	8h				
						Act. W	8h				
3		− Identify Stakeholders	8 hrs	1.38 days	Tue 7/3	Work		5h		3h	
						Act. W		5h			
	📝	*Prudence Project*	*8 hrs*		Tue 7/3	Work		5h		3h	
						Act. W		5h			
4		− Select Project Team	32 hrs	4 days	Thu 7/5	Work				9.2h	11.6h
						Act. W					

Note that the actual hours (5 hours in the above example) are rolled-up for the task and the remaining work (3 hours) is scheduled for the following day (Project assumes that the time you have entered is "as at" the end of the day). There is also an edited symbol placed in the Task Information box and, as usual, placing your cursor over the symbol will pop-up the relevant details.

3		− Identify Stakeholders	8 hrs	1.38 days	Tue 7/3/07
	📝	*Prudence Project*	*8 hrs*		Tue 7/3/07
		📝 This assignment work has been edited.			
4			32 hrs	4 days	Thu 7/5/07

Percentage Completed

There is a certain amount of risk involved in using percentage completed as the measure of work done on a task. It is human nature for most people to be optimistic about their progress, so a measure of actual work done and an estimate of work still to be completed is usually more accurate. However, it will sometimes be appropriate to use percentage completed where it is not practical to track work more closely.

1 Open your project in Task Sheet view and select View>Table>Tracking from the menu bar

	Task Name	Act. Start	Act. Finish	% Comp.	Phys. % Comp.	Act. Dur.	Rem. Dur.	Act. Cost	Act. Work
1	− Initiation Stage	Mon 7/2/07	NA	13%	0%	1.95 days	13.05 days	$520.00	13 hrs
2	Agree Project Objectives	Mon 7/2/07	Mon 7/2/07	100%	0%	1 day	0 days	$320.00	8 hrs
3	Identify Stakeholders	Tue 7/3/07	NA	73%	0%	1 day	0.38 days	$200.00	5 hrs
4	Select Project Team	NA	NA	0%	0%	0 days	4 days	$0.00	0 hrs
5	Identify Business Case	NA	NA	0%	0%	0 days	2 days	$0.00	0 hrs
6	Analyze the Risks	NA	NA	0%	0%	0 days	1 day	$0.00	0 hrs
7	Produce Outline Project Plan	NA	NA	0%	0%	0 days	1 day	$0.00	0 hrs
8	Project Approval	NA	NA	0%	0%	0 days	5 days	$0.00	0 hrs

2 Select View>Toolbars>Tracking from the Menu bar to open the tracking toolbar

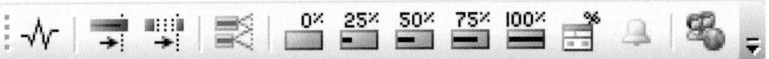

3 Update the percentage completed for tasks by typing it into the % Comp field or use the 25%, 50%, 75% buttons on the tracking toolbar if appropriate

4 Select View>Gantt Chart from the menu bar to switch back to Gantt chart view and note the part completed tasks will have incomplete completion bars through them

You can continue to update tasks as completed or part completed in Gantt chart view using the tracking toolbar.

Duration Completed

You can enter the actual and remaining duration for a task in a similar way to the way you can enter actual work done.

1 In Gantt Chart view select the task you want to enter duration information for

2 Click the Update Tasks button (on the tracking toolbar) to open the Update Tasks dialog box

3 Type in the actual duration to date, the remaining duration and click OK to update the task

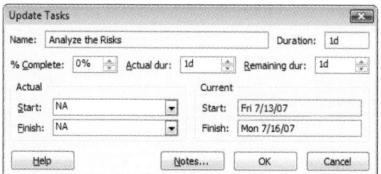

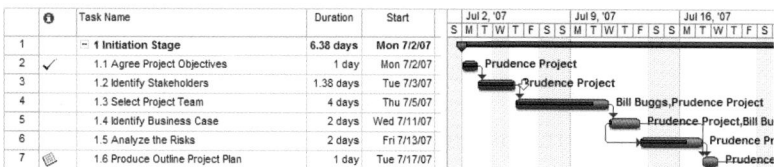

4 Click the Update Tasks button again and note that the Percentage complete and Actual start date have now been updated in line with the actual and remaining duration

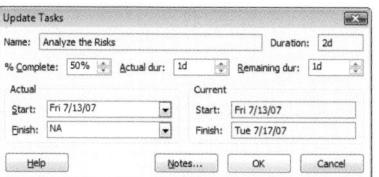

As well as updating duration, the Update Tasks dialog box can also be used to update the percentage completed and the actual start and finish dates. Changes made to any of these fields will update the other fields as appropriate to keep the task details correct.

In the same way, the actual and remaining duration can also be edited directly in the Task Sheet Tracking view as used in the Percentage Completed topic on the previous page. There are often several ways of doing the same thing in Project.

Entering Costs

Project will normally calculate costs for you based on the actual work involved in the task and the cost details you entered for the resource assigned to the task. However, you can also enter actual cost details directly.

1 Select Tools> Options from the Menu bar and select the Calculation tab

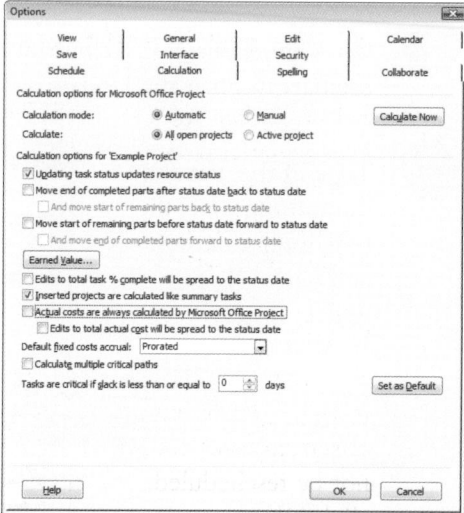

2 Clear the "Actual costs are always calculated by Microsoft Office Project" check box and click OK

3 In Task Usage view select View Table>Tracking from the Menu bar

4 Select Format>Details>Actual Cost from the Menu bar

5 Now select the Actual Cost field for the relevant task and resource and enter the actual cost (as illustrated below)

	Task Name	Act. Start	Act. Finish	Details	T	F	S	S	Jul 16, '07 M	T
6	– Analyze the Risks	Fri 7/13/07	NA	Work		5h			8h	3h
				Act. Work		5h			3h	
				Act. Cost		$300.00	$0.00	$0.00	$120.00	
	Prudence Project	Fri 7/13/07	NA	Work		5h			8h	3h
				Act. Work		5h			3h	
				Act. Cost		$300.00	$0.00	$0.00	$120.00	

While it is possible to enter all resource costs in this manner, it would become fairly time consuming. On the whole it is far simpler to let Project calculate resource costs for you as you can vary the rate for different types of work (as covered in Variable Resource Costs, Cost Rate Tables and Applying Resource Rates in chapter 8).

Updating as Scheduled

If you have one or more tasks that have been started and/or completed in line with your schedule, you can use the Update as Scheduled button on the tracking toolbar or the Update Project dialog box (Tools>Tracking>Update Project).

1   In Gantt Chart view click the Update As Scheduled button on the tracking toolbar

2   Select Update work as completed through, select the date you want all tasks updated to and click OK

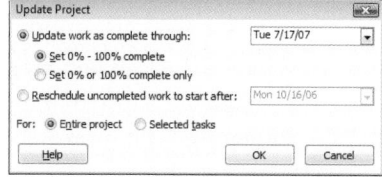

3   If you receive a Planning Wizard warning that some unstarted tasks could not be rescheduled, click OK to continue and update the Gantt chart (you can check the constraints on the relevant tasks later)

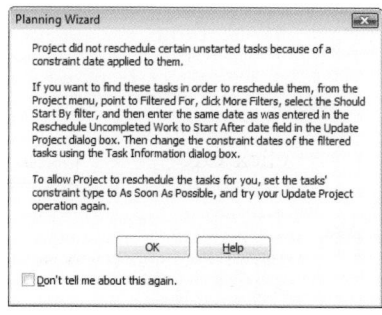

In the example above, the Gantt chart shows tasks up to 1.5 fully complete and Task 1.6 as partially complete. As can be seen (right) the task actually completes 1 day later than the

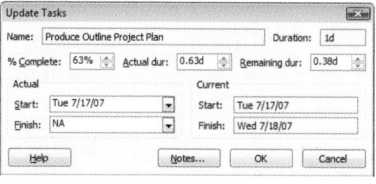

date selected at Step 2 and the percentage completed, actual and remaining duration have all been adjusted accordingly.

Actual v Baseline

Having set the project baseline, you can monitor your actual progress against this baseline at any time. The baseline and actual figures can be displayed in a number of tables and through the use of Tracking Gantt Chart view.

As an example we will increase the actual work on a task and view the results.

1 In Gantt Chart view, select a task and use the Update Task dialog box to increase the actual and remaining duration

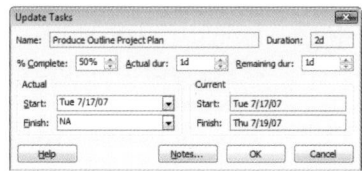

2 Select View>Table>Work from the Menu bar to open the Work Table

	Task Name	Work	Baseline	Variance	Actual	Remaining	% W. Comp.
1	− 1 Initiation Stage	112 hrs	80 hrs	32 hrs	104 hrs	8 hrs	93%
2	1.1 Agree Project Objectives	8 hrs	8 hrs	0 hrs	8 hrs	0 hrs	100%
3	1.2 Identify Stakeholders	8 hrs	8 hrs	0 hrs	8 hrs	0 hrs	100%
4	1.3 Select Project Team	32 hrs	32 hrs	0 hrs	32 hrs	0 hrs	100%
5	1.4 Identify Business Case	32 hrs	16 hrs	16 hrs	32 hrs	0 hrs	100%
6	1.5 Analyze the Risks	16 hrs	8 hrs	8 hrs	16 hrs	0 hrs	100%
7	1.6 Produce Outline Project Plan	16 hrs	8 hrs	8 hrs	8 hrs	8 hrs	50%
8	1.7 Project Approval	0 hrs	0 hrs	0 hrs	0 hrs	0 hrs	0%

Note in Table View that Work = Actual + Remaining and that Variance = Work - Baseline.

In the example above we have used background cell highlighting (page 159) to highlight the variances (this is not an automatic feature of Project).

3 Select View>Table Cost to display the actual and baseline cost and View>Table>Variance to see the start and finish date variance (highlighted below)

	Task Name	Start	Finish	Baseline Start	Baseline Finish	Start Var.	Finish Var.
1	− 1 Initiation Stage	Mon 7/2/07	Thu 7/26/07	Mon 7/2/07	Mon 7/23/07	0 days	2.38 days
2	1.1 Agree Project Objectives	Mon 7/2/07	Mon 7/2/07	Mon 7/2/07	Mon 7/2/07	0 days	0 days
3	1.2 Identify Stakeholders	Tue 7/3/07	Thu 7/5/07	Tue 7/3/07	Tue 7/3/07	0 days	0.38 days
4	1.3 Select Project Team	Thu 7/5/07	Wed 7/11/07	Thu 7/5/07	Tue 7/10/07	0.38 days	0.38 days
5	1.4 Identify Business Case	Wed 7/11/07	Fri 7/13/07	Wed 7/11/07	Thu 7/12/07	0.38 days	0.38 days
6	1.5 Analyze the Risks	Fri 7/13/07	Tue 7/17/07	Fri 7/13/07	Fri 7/13/07	0.38 days	1.38 days
7	1.6 Produce Outline Project Plan	Tue 7/17/07	Thu 7/19/07	Mon 7/16/07	Mon 7/16/07	1.38 days	2.38 days

Tracking Gantt Chart

The Tracking Gantt Chart view gives a graphical representation of the actual state of the project compared to the baseline.

 Select View>Tracking Gantt Chart from the Menu bar to display the Tracking Gantt Chart

	❶	Task Name	Duration	Start	Jul 2, '07	Jul 9, '07	Jul 16, '07	Jul 23, '07
1		− Initiation Stage	7.38 days	Mon 7/2/07				65%
2	✓	Agree Project Objectives	1 day	Mon 7/2/07	100%			
3	✓	Identify Stakeholders	1.38 days	Tue 7/3/07	100%			
4	✓	Select Project Team	4 days	Thu 7/5/07		100%		
5	✓	Identify Business Case	2 days	Wed 7/11/07		100%		
6	✓	Analyze the Risks	2 days	Fri 7/13/07			100%	
7	✎	Produce Outline Project Plan	2 days	Tue 7/17/07			50%	
8		Project Approval	5 days	Thu 7/19/07				◇ 7/26
9		− Strategy Stage	7.63 days	Thu 7/26/07				
10		− Carry Out Interviews	5 days	Thu 7/26/07				
11		Interview Managers	2 days	Thu 7/26/07				

Note in the example above:

- Actual stage progress is shown as a hatched line below the stage summary bar at the top

- Percentage completed is displayed to the right of started and completed task bars and summary task bars

- The baseline task bars are displayed (black and white shaded) below the actual and schedule task bars

- Outline numbering does not appear in Tracking Gantt Chart view

- Completed tasks (actual) are displayed with a blue task bar

- Scheduled tasks (not yet started) are displayed with a red (if on the critical path) or blue shaded task bar

- Started but not completed tasks are displayed with a red (if on the critical path) or blue part shaded task bar

- Baseline milestones are displayed as black and white diamonds

- Overall the project is 2.38 days behind the baseline schedule

As the example project has a 5 day lag time between Producing the Outline Project Plan and the Project Approval milestone, we could, with the project sponsor's agreement, reduce this lag time to bring the project back on schedule.

Hot tip

Building in some lag time allows you to cope with task delays without ruining the schedule.

Progress Lines

Progress Lines can be drawn on the Gantt Chart or Tracking Gantt Chart views at any date to show the actual or expected progress as at that date.

They work by linking the tasks that are scheduled to be started, in progress or completed on that date. Tasks that are behind schedule result in peaks to the left of the line and tasks that are ahead of schedule result in peaks to the right of the line.

1 In Gantt Chart or Tracking Gantt Chart view, click the Add Progress Line button on the Tracking Toolbar

2 The cursor will change to a jagged line with a left and right arrow, move this over the Gantt chart and a Progress Line pop-up box will be displayed

Progress Line	
Progress Date:	Fri 7/20/07
Click the mouse to display a progress line on this date	

3 Once you have the desired date in the progress line pop-up box, click and the progress line will be displayed on the Gantt chart

In the example above, the progress line has been shown as at Friday July 20 and at that date one task (Produce Outline Project Plan) is scheduled to be completed but is not yet completed. Also the milestone Project Approval (to which we allocated a 5-day duration) is scheduled to have started but has not yet done so.

4 To remove the progress line, double-click on it, to open the Progress Line dialog box, click on Delete and click on OK and the progress line will be removed again

Closing a Project

As the project progresses it will eventually be time to think about closing the project. This is obviously a significant event and should be planned as part of the final (Implementation) stage.

Formal Project End

Once the project is formally closed, all the data will be available on time, costs and resource usage, so the final results of the project can be documented and published.

Project Deliverables

While all the major deliverables should have been completed, it is not unusual to find that some project deliverables have been left incomplete, for whatever reason. Checking and confirming all deliverables, will ensure they have all been completed.

Support Arrangements

Once the project is closed the project team are released and any required support arrangements for the business should have been identified and implemented.

Lessons Learned

There will normally be a lot of lessons learned during the course of a project. From the business point of view, it is essential that these lessons are not lost. While the project manager might well remember and benefit from them in future, it is also important that the whole business does too. Therefore, any lessons learned during the project (however painful) should be documented.

Benefit Assessment

Once the project is closed and the full costs known, the business benefits that it actually results in can be measured over a suitable period of time, for later evaluation by the business.

End Project Report

The main deliverables from Project Closure will be the end project report. This should build on the documented end stage reports and summarize the final results of the project. In addition to the project performance against time, cost and resource usage, the end project report should also document the lessons learned, the on-going support arrangements and any follow on recommendations.

Finally it gives the project manager the chance to thank the members of the project team for their work on the project.

Summary

- Once you have scheduled your project and allocated resources, you need to start tracking the actual progress against schedule

- Capture progress information, ideally once a week, on tasks started and completed, hours worked and hours remaining

- Completed work can be entered by putting the finish date into the Update Tasks dialog box

- Part completed work can be input as hours worked and hours remaining to completion in Task Usage view

- The easiest way of inputting part completed work (although the least accurate) is to set the percentage complete in Task Sheet view or use the percentage buttons on the Tracking toolbar

- Duration completed and remaining duration can be input using the Update Tasks dialog box

- Actual costs of work completed can be entered in Task Usage view, but generally it is easier to allow Project to calculate the cost of work from the resource information

- Updating as scheduled is a quick way of entering progress information if tasks are being completed to schedule

- Actual progress can be compared to baseline using the Work, Cost and Variance tables in Gantt Chart view

- Tracking Gantt Chart view gives you a view of actual and scheduled tasks superimposed over the baseline

- Budget tracking can be done by task or resource by applying the Cost table and in summary for stages and the complete project by showing the project summary task

- Project statistics gives you a summary view of current project progress against baseline

- Progress lines can add a visual indication of the state of the project at any point in time

- Project closure should be used to document the final results of the project and capture lessons learned for the future

Index